Then
&Now

JAZZ
Then
&Now

BY DAVID LEE FISH Ph.D

intune PARTNERS

Distributed by Hal Leonard Corporation

Copyright © 2011 by David Lee Fish Ph.D

Published in 2011 by In Tune Partners
582 North Broadway
White Plains, NY 10603

Distributed by Hal Leonard Corporation
7777 West Bluemound Road
Milwaukee, WI 53213

Cover Photos: Louis Armstrong, Library of Congress Prints and Photographs Division, New York World-Telegram and the Sun Newspaper Photograph Collection; Wynton Marsalis, Clay Patrick McBride at Anderson Hopkins. Every reasonable effort has been made to contact copyright holders and secure permissions. Omissions can be remedied in future editions.

Printed in the United States of America

Editorial Director: Emile Menasche
Book Design: Jackie Jordan

Library of Congress Cataloging-in-Publication Data is available upon request.

ISBN: 978-1-61774-232-3

musicalive.com

To the memory of Don Ellis

CONTENTS

ACKNOWLEDGMENTS

From the Author

I would like to thank my mentors, without whom this book would not have been possible. They include Trent Kynaston, William Malm, and Joan Boucher. Thanks also go to the publisher, In Tune Partners, especially its CEO, Irwin Kornfeld, and editorial director, Emile D. Menasché.

From the Publisher

Special thanks to: Clare Cerullo and Carol Flannery at Hal Leonard Performing Arts Publishing Group; editor Adam Perlmutter and designer Jackie Jordan at In Tune Partners; Dr. Bruce Boyd Raeburn and Alaina W. Hébert, Hogan Jazz Archive at Tulane University; Genevieve Sansom Stewart, Wynton Marsalis Enterprises; Scott Thompson, Jazz at Lincoln Center; and Toby Silver, Tom Tierney, and Che Williams from Sony Music Entertainment, Inc., for helping provide many of the pictures in this book.

Big Bad Voodoo Daddy

WHAT'S ALL THIS JAZZ ABOUT?

It had been a hot, end-of-summer day in Chicago. The first Friday of September, it marked the beginning of a long Labor Day weekend. The New York Yankees were in town but had lost against the Cubs at Wrigley Field. By the evening, the temperature was starting to cool off. Things were just starting to heat up in Millennium Park on the shore of Lake Michigan, though.

Millennium Park's Jay Pritzker Pavilion simmered with the sounds of the 32nd Chicago Jazz Festival. The event started as a casual affair in 1974 to remember the recent death of legendary jazz composer and bandleader Duke Ellington. Since then, it has grown into a major annual festival for the city organized by the Mayor's Office of Special Events.

This particular evening at the Chicago Jazz Festival started with a set played by the Lincoln Park High School Jazz Ensemble, one of the best student bands in the city. A new group, the

Noteworthy Jazz Ensemble, made up of local music teachers, joined them on the pavilion stage. The audience enjoyed seeing the present and future of jazz making music together.

Next came James Dapogny and his Chicago Jazz Band. A music scholar and an emeritus professor at the University of Michigan, Dapogny has made a name for himself by specializing in a style of jazz that flourished in Chicago some eighty years ago. Artists like Louis Armstrong and King Oliver gave birth to Chicago jazz in the 1920s. Dapogny keeps it alive.

At 70, Dapogny is a veteran jazz artist. The night's featured performer had that beat, though. The highlight of the festival was a 75th birthday bash for Chicago's native son Ramsey Lewis. A renowned jazz artist, Lewis recorded a number of million-selling crossover songs in the 1960s on the electric piano. He went on to have a distinguished carrier in jazz, and this was a night to celebrate it.

The 32nd Chicago Jazz Festival provides us with a great view of jazz in the early part of the 21st century. It is an art form that respects the past but lives in the present. It is a living tradition that has taken a number of forms over the years. These represent streams making up a river of music that keeps on flowing into the future.

Jazz first developed in the Storyville section of New Orleans in the first decades of the 20th century. It was wonderfully infectious music filled with syncopated beats and an unheard of degree of improvisation. As catchy as it was, no one could have imagined that it would go onto to become America's music. Even more remarkable is the fact that it became so influential around the world.

Actually, though, it is little surprise that jazz became so important. Someone once said that jazz *is* what America aspires *to be*. We find in it the ideals that we cherish as Americans. Jazz musicians work together to create something fresh and original. They do so through the spontaneous interaction of their individual creativity. *E pluribus unum* (Out of many, one.) That is America. That is jazz.

Jazz has indeed taken on a variety of forms in its long history. In this book, we will learn about how the language has evolved over the years, and about the traits that tie today's jazz to its historical roots. Along the way, we'll meet memorable artists with nicknames like Satchmo, Bird, Dizzy, Prez, and Cannonball.

Like most history books, this one follows a fairly straight path through the years. We begin with a look at the music that influenced the development of traditional jazz. In doing so, we consider the musical characteristics of jazz's African and European roots and how these appear in American forms that predate jazz, like ragtime and the blues.

We then travel to New Orleans to witness the birth of jazz. We arrive just in time for the opening of the city's Storyville section, which will play a major role in the development of traditional jazz. While in New Orleans, we meet the first pioneers of jazz, including King Oliver and Louis Armstrong. We journey with them to Chicago and beyond as they spread jazz after the closing of Storyville.

Our next chapter pauses to consider the artistry of Louis Armstrong, the first musical genius of jazz. We learn that he, more than anyone, helped the music grow stylistically beyond New Orleans. In particular, we observe his role in the development of a new rhythmic orientation for jazz, swing.

We enjoy a ringside seat in Chapter 4 to watch spark a musical craze that seized America in the years just before the World War II. This brings us up to the Harlem section of New York City in the 1930s to hear a legendary swing band, the one led by drummer Chick Webb at the Savoy Ballroom. We then watch as Benny Goodman and other white bandleaders take Webb's musical ideas and help them cross lines of color in American society.

Two members of the jazz nobility, Duke Ellington and Count Basie, reigned in the kingdom of swing in the 1930s and beyond. In Chapter 5, we learn of their important contributions. Both served as longtime leaders of great jazz orchestras. We also see how Ellington developed as one of the finest and most serious composers to come from the world of jazz.

We enter the world of modern jazz with Chapter 6. We find bebop architects like Charlie Parker and Dizzy Gillespie heating things up in late-night jam sessions at small nightclubs. Their musical explorations brought a new approach to the music, one that remains the basic foundation for the music even today.

Chapter 7 takes us on an exploration of jazz as an avenue for vocalists. While there, we linger a while to consider the music of Ella Fitzgerald and Billie Holiday. We then travel south of the border in Chapter 8 to learn how Cuban and Brazilian sounds influenced the development of Latin jazz.

Returning home in Chapter 9, we see how some jazz artists in the late 1940s and beyond sought relief from the hot tempos and assertive playing of bebop. They found it in the more temperate climes of cool jazz. We next reflect on the contributions of two more giants of jazz in Chapter 10. We watch Miles Davis emerge from the bebop combo of Charlie Parker to become an important bandleader in his own right. We also observe him as a key pioneer in several stylistic movements, including cool jazz. We then

follow John Coltrane as he, in turn, emerges from Miles Davis' band to help jazz take giant steps forward.

Moving into the 1970s with Chapter 11, we find another of the movements that Davis pioneered. Fusion served up a blend of jazz with rock and funk grooves that seemed to eclipse swing-oriented jazz for much of the decade. In Chapter 12, what became known as straight-ahead jazz returns to the scene with the jazz revival of the 1980s. We end our musical journey with a look at jazz today in Chapter 13.

While the chapters of this book are laid out chronologically, feel free to jump in anywhere you feel inspired to, as each chapter stands fairly well on its own. This allows you to enjoy the story of jazz, then and now following your own path if you prefer.   However you proceed, you will come to understand what is perhaps the most fundamental thing about jazz. In the words of documentary film producer Ken Burns, "The genius of our country is improvisation, and jazz reflects that. It's our great contribution to the arts."

Scott Joplin

WHAT IS AMERICAN MUSIC?

American music takes many forms. There is music of both the white and black church. There is marching band music heard on the Fourth of July and at school football games. There is the music of Broadway musicals and Hollywood movies. There are also all sorts of dance forms, from the cakewalk of the 19th century to the hip-hop of today. And that is just the short list.

Jazz is often referred to as *the* American music. It developed during the 20th century, as America was becoming a modern country. Jazz became the soundtrack of this time. Something about it just seemed to capture the vibrancy of American culture as it confidently moved forward.

But nothing comes from nothing. That is to say, everything is born of something else. We can certainly say it about jazz. As you'll see, the form developed from earlier types of American music. These blended together to create something distinctly new with jazz. The earlier forms themselves grew from their own roots. For most, these origins lay an ocean away, in Europe or Africa.

The African and European Roots of Jazz

All music is folk music. I ain't never heard a horse sing a song. —LOUIS ARMSTRONG

Africa is a large continent with over 800 ethnic groups. Each has its own language, religion and distinct way of life. African music, even within certain regions, is equally diverse. To a West African, the musical styles of the Ewe of Ghana and the Mandé of Mali are very different—as different as rock 'n' roll and hip-hop are to us.

West Africa has had a large influence on music in the United States. For over 200 years, traders forcibly brought West African slaves to America. They came from some 45 ethnic groups. Most were sold as workers to plantation owners in Southern states. By 1860, four million toiled the fields and performed other manual labor. They endured brutal imprisonment, endless work, and miserable poverty.

Slave owners tried to extinguish almost every aspect of African culture. They forbade language, religion, and other native ways, including music. The owners did not even allow slaves to keep or recreate African instruments. They believed the slaves could secretly communicate through drumming.

African ways of making music survived in the United States regardless, through adaptation of and blending with Euro-American traditions. For example, slaves heard Bible stories and learned church hymns at revivals and camp meetings attended by both whites and blacks.

Camp meetings led to the conversion of many slaves to Christianity. It also had an unexpected consequence. Slaves developed the music of the meetings into a distinctly African-American form, the spiritual, which we'll learn more about later.

While there is much diversity in the music of West Africa, African traditions combined in slave culture to produce a number of common characteristics. These can still be heard in the musical traditions that have sprung from African-American culture. Genres from jazz and blues to soul and hip-hop bear the mark of West African music.

FASCINATING RHYTHMS

Rhythm is the most obvious West African trait heard in African-American forms. We can trace this to the importance of drumming in West Africa, where some ensembles are made up entirely of percussion instruments. This is almost unheard of in traditional European music.

Each percussion instrument in a West African ensemble typically plays a repeating rhythmic pattern. When performed together, these patterns create sophisticated layers of sound that interact rhythmically with one another in complex ways, creating a kaleidoscope of sound. To the untrained ear, such *polyrhythms*—more than one rhythm at once—can sound like a jumble of rhythm.

Rhythm is also important in most forms of African-American music. However, it does not usually contain the same level of complexity as found in Africa. We instead hear the essence of polyrhythms in something called *syncopation*—rhythmic accentuation of musically weak beats and/or offbeat accents.

To understand syncopation, think of the Christmas song "Jingle Bells." The beat pattern of much traditional European and Euro-American music is *one*-and, *two*-and, *one*-and, *two*-and, etc., with each beat 1 being strongly accented; beat 2, less accented; and the upbeats (the "ands"), unaccented. You can feel this rhythm by clapping on the 1 and 2 downbeats and saying "and" on the upbeats. Say *one* louder than *two* and whisper the "ands."

The way we normally sing "Jingle Bells" neatly fits this pattern of accented and unaccented beats: *Jin*-gle **bells,** *Jin*-gle **bells**, *Jin*-gle **all** the *way*. The syllable *jin* and the word *way* fall on beat 1. **Bell** and **all** are on beat 2, while the syllable "gle" and the word "the" happen on the upbeats.

LIVES AND TIMES

Emancipation Abraham Lincoln signed an executive order in 1863 proclaiming the freedom of millions of American slaves. With this act and the Union victory some two years later, all slaves gained their freedom. Reconstruction and the Jim Crow laws it brought spelled inequality for most blacks for another century.

Phonograph Edison's invention of the phonograph in 1877 changed the world of music forever, allowing people to listen to renowned performers in the comfort of their own homes. The full development of jazz would hardly have been possible without it.

Ragtime During the 1890s, black pianists in the Midwest began blending African-American musical forms like the cakewalk with the sounds of military marches popular then. They called the results rags. Composer Scott Joplin enjoyed a national hit with his ragtime composition "Maple Leaf Rag." Ragtime spread to New Orleans and influenced the birth of jazz.

Let's now jazz up "Jingle Bells" a little by adding some syncopation to it. We'll keep the basic *one*-and, *two*-and rhythmic pattern. While we clap this however, we can change the accents of the melody to stress the upbeats. Jin-**gle** bells, Jin-**gle** bells, Jin-**gle** all **the** way.

We could even create more syncopation by delaying or pushing some of the notes of the melody so they fall between the downbeats and upbeats. For example, you could wait until just after beat 1 to sing the syllable *jin*.

Now we're syncopating. It may seem like we are putting the emphasis on the "wrong" syllable. Instead, we are creating a dynamic interplay—tension between the basic beat and the melody.

Syncopation is one of the most obvious characteristics of black American music that finds its roots in West Africa. Most of the musical traditions that have come from the black community contain heaping helpings of it. Jazz is certainly one of these traditions.

MORE WEST AFRICAN INFLUENCES

Other West African musical traits also found their way to America. One is known as call and response. This typically involves a leader singing or playing a phrase of music (the call) and then another performer answering it (the response). The response might be the same phrase or a complementary one. While an individual typically performs the call, the response could be either by an individual or a group.

We find call and response in many American musical traditions having roots in Africa. You hear it when a leader calls out the next line for a gospel choir to sing. You hear it when a bluesman answers a phrase he has just sung with a lick on his guitar. You hear it in jazz when an accompanying musician echoes a phrase improvised by a soloist.

West African styles of singing also came to America. In traditional European music, ***bel canto*** ("beautiful singing") is an important ideal. It emphasizes a consistent, full sound on all notes and stresses vowels over consonants. Think of Italian opera and you get the idea. Singing in West Africa uses the voice in a more varied way. A singer will shout, whisper, growl, yodel, and glide from one note to the next.

We can find all of these vocal traits in African-American forms. The raspy, shouting style of many soul singers is a good example. Their art owes more to West Africa than it does to the *bel canto* tradition. The same goes for the falsetto shouts of rock 'n' roll pioneer Little Richard and the aching croak of jazz legend Billie Holiday.

The place of music in West African society finds echoes in America as well. Rather than an elevated art, it is more part of daily life, involving almost everyone. A group of workers might spontaneously break out in rhythm to cancel stamps at a post office or construct a building. A family might sing, play percussion instruments, and dance to celebrate a child bringing home a good report card from school.

We can clearly see this same attitude in black American churches. There, the congregation participates extensively in the music making; almost everyone spontaneously joins in. Similarly, young jazz musicians are often encouraged to sit in during performances, and audiences are free to clap along and shout approval.

JAZZ DANCE

This leads us to a final West African trait that has enriched music in America—a close relationship between music and the other arts, especially dance. While music is related to dance everywhere in the world, African musicians often dance as they perform. When you watch Cab Calloway, James Brown, Michael Jackson, or Beyoncé sing and dance, you are seeing a clear reflection of West African tradition.

Jazz and the other musical forms that have sprung from the African-American experience clearly show the mark of these characteristics. What makes them distinct, though, is that they have also incorporated European elements. Jazz may be enliv-

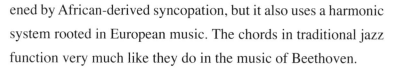

ened by African-derived syncopation, but it also uses a harmonic system rooted in European music. The chords in traditional jazz function very much like they do in the music of Beethoven.

European instruments are also the mainstay of jazz and other musical forms that originated from black Americans. The trumpet, clarinet, saxophone, tuba, piano, string bass, and guitar, as well as the cymbal, snare, and bass drum, all come from Europe.

However, the playing style of these instruments changed in jazz, soul, and other African-American traditions. For example, a jazz saxophonist is free to color the sound coming from his horn with a variety of techniques. She can growl, squawk, shriek, and more. In this way, the playing is like African and African-American singing.

Some European and Euro-American musical forms also influenced African-American music. Musically talented slaves played at parties held by their masters. For such occasions, they learned European dance styles such as the jig. Black Americans continued to absorb musics rooted in European tradition after emancipation. In particular, Euro-American song forms influenced black musicians.

SUGGESTED LISTENING

SCOTT JOPLIN
"Maple Leaf Rag"

ROBERT JOHNSON
"Sweet Home Chicago"

Early African-American Music

We have absolutely no reason to worry about lack of positive and affirmative philosophy. It's built in us. The phrasing, the sound of the music attest this fact. —JOHN COLTRANE

Jazz developed directly out of the African-American musical forms that preceded it. To understand its roots, we must therefore consider these traditions. As we will see, they enriched the lives of black Americans in both the slave and post-slave periods of our history.

Little is known about the earliest African-American music since it comes from the period of slavery, which predates the invention of audio recording. Also, those making the music neither wrote it down nor wrote about it. For their part, slave owners and outside observers also seemed to take little notice.

The Old Plantation, an American folk art watercolor

We do know that spirituals borrowed the sort of Euro-American melodies sung at camp meetings. However, the singing style and the clapped accompaniment apparently sounded much more African. Spirituals also sometimes served different ends than the music of camp meetings.

For one thing, spirituals accompanied religious dances called ring shouts that find their direct roots in Africa. They may have also been used as a type of veiled protest against slavery. The lyrics of some even seem to give directions on how to escape captivity.

MINSTREL SHOWS AND CAKEWALKS

Minstrel shows give us a few more clues about black music of the slave period. These were originally part of a white theatrical tradition that dealt in black stereotypes. Minstrel shows lampooned slave life in demeaning and racist ways. However, they still patterned their music and dance after black traditions.

After the Civil War, black performers started appearing in minstrel shows as well. By the 1900s, the tradition actually became one of black artists performing for black audiences. Genuine African-American music found its way into minstrel shows as this happened. From the 1870s, for example, upbeat spirituals known as jubilees started appearing. So did cakewalks.

The cakewalk actually dates from the period of slavery. Couples would strut around in a square before judges, and the best dancers would then receive a cake as a prize. Taken up by black minstrelsy, the cakewalk became a popular staged dance. The music of the late 19th century cakewalk was in a lively, syncopated two-step rhythm.

Ragtime and the Blues

When I'm dead 25 years, people are going to begin to recognize me. —SCOTT JOPLIN

A craze for a new musical form called ragtime swept America in 1899. "Maple Leaf Rag," a hit instrumental piece, was the match that lit the fire. Ragtime would reign as America's most popular music for over a decade. It was only dethroned after 1917 when a newer music came along. Interestingly, the newcomer, jazz, took much of its inspiration from ragtime.

Ragtime grew out of several musical influences. One was

the music of the cakewalk. Another was the jig as performed by black musicians for dances. Both of these styles included a significant amount of syncopation, which they handed on to ragtime. Military marches also had a strong influence on ragtime.

The form had humble beginnings. Ragtime seems to have first developed in the saloons of Midwest cities like St. Louis. This was in the last decade or so of the 19th century. Ragtime pianists spread it from there as they travelled up and down the Mississippi River.

SCOTT JOPLIN AND HIS RAGS

Ragtime fascinated a young black musician who wanted to become a concert pianist and composer of serious music. Scott Joplin (1868–1917) lived at the time in Sedalia, Missouri and

had studied music in college. Joplin used his musical training to take ragtime beyond its roots, turning it into finely crafted compositions.

Joplin's "Maple Leaf Rag" was so commercially successful that it sold over a million copies in sheet music form—the mp3 of that time. The composition's appeal came in large part from sounding like a syncopated march. This gave it a lilt that must have sounded like a fresh take on the military music that was so popular at the turn of the century. It allowed ragtime to cross over racial lines to become accepted by Americans of all color.

"Maple Leaf Rag" is indeed a finely crafted work. Some even refer to it as an example of a "classical rag." Whether we consider it art or popular music, "Maple Leaf Rag" is infectious. Its catchy melodies prance above striding bass lines; its syncopation immediately sets feet tapping and heads bobbing.

No other ragtime composer enjoyed Joplin's level of success. Long after his death, a number of his rags remain popular. Joplin continued to hold high musical ideals throughout his career. In 1902, he published a ballet suite that incorporated ragtime elements. His crowning achievement was a three-act opera, "Treemonisha," completed in 1910.

THE BLUES

We will look at how ragtime influenced the birth of jazz in the next chapter. For now, let's consider another African-American music that helped give rise to jazz—the blues.

The origins of the blues are shrouded in much mystery. While no one knows exactly where or when it first developed, it was likely at about the same time ragtime was emerging. Whatever its exact origins, the blues grew out of a number of musical forms that were common among black Americans after the Civil War. These included the free-rhythm field hollers of sharecroppers and the rhythmic work songs sung by groups of laborers.

Early blues is closely associated with the Yazoo Delta in the Southern state of Mississippi. Sometime around the turn of the 20th century, guitar-wielding bluesmen started performing at dances in Mississippi towns and at juke joints near the vast cotton plantations of the Delta.

The music of these bluesmen was strikingly different. First, it relied on a new musical form. Most popular music, then and now, is built on eight-measure stanzas, with each measure having four beats. These stanzas typically each contain two lyrical phrases, which we label A and B.

In the blues, the A phrase of each stanza is repeated. This results in an AAB structure and stanzas that are 12 measures or bars in length. You may have heard of 12-bar blues before. That is its meaning.

Here are the lyrics to the first stanza of "Sweet Home Chicago" by renowned Delta bluesman Robert Johnson (1911–1938) (who was apparently much better at music than geography). It follows the AAB lyrical structure just described:

> *Oh, baby, don't you want to go*
> *Oh, baby, don't you want to go*
> *To the land of California, sweet home Chicago*

The melody in a blues song like "Sweet Home Chicago" also uses a distinctive scale. This so-called blues scale is *pentatonic*, meaning it contains five basic pitches. A lot of European and Euro-American folk songs also use pentatonic scales.

However, the blues scale is different than the pentatonic scales found in such folksongs. It is essentially a minor scale that is typically sung or played over a major chord. This creates a fascinating dissonance between melody and harmony that helps define the blues.

The second note of the blues scales has a particularly biting quality. It is actually known as the blue note. You can hear it on the word *baby* in Johnson's 1936 recording of "Sweet Home Chicago." A bluesman like Johnson often increases the effect of this blues note by purposely singing it somewhat off key.

As we will see in the next chapter, jazz has embraced the blues since its infancy. Some of the earliest jazz recordings not only have the word blues in their title but use the 12-bar blues form and its characteristic scale. A close relationship between the blues and jazz continues to this day.

The Legacy of American Roots Music

Some of the African-American musical traditions that gave rise to the blues are now little more than museum pieces. Practically no one dances the cakewalk or sings field hollers anymore. While they may be revisited occasionally, spirituals and ragtime have also faded as popular forms.

The blues is a different story. It has enjoyed a long existence and can be heard today at clubs and festivals across the country. In part, it survived because it has adapted to evolving times and tastes, all the while staying true to its essence.

Jazz would not exist at all if not for the influence of earlier African-American musical traditions. Two were especially important. As you'll see in the next chapter, ragtime and the blues blended with the strong brass band tradition of New Orleans to create something new. While the story is more than ragtime plus blues equals jazz, it is impossible to imagine it having formed without them.

Jelly Roll Morton

CHAPTER 2

TRADITIONAL JAZZ

Jazz has gone through many stylistic changes over the years. From the swing of the 1930s to the noise-jazz of today, a number of types of jazz have developed. In between, there has been bebop, Latin jazz, cool jazz, hard bop, modal jazz, fusion, and more. Traditional jazz refers to the original form of the music—the taproot from which all others have come.

Major musical developments tend to emanate from specific places at particular times. This is certainly true for the birth of jazz. History books tell us the music first developed in New Orleans during the early decades of the 20th century. It makes jazz the product of a distinct period in the history of one of America's most fascinating cities. We need to understand New Orleans then to appreciate this music.

In learning about traditional jazz, we will meet a number of talented and colorful figures who helped give birth to the music.

We'll learn about artists with nicknames like Jelly Roll, Bunk, King, and Kid and look at how some of them migrated north to Chicago and elsewhere, taking jazz with them. As they journeyed, they made jazz the most popular music in the country.

New Orleans

I think that I may say that an American has not seen the United States until he has seen Mardi-Gras in New Orleans. —MARK TWAIN

New Orleans is a city quite unlike any other in America. It sits along the Gulf of Mexico at the mouth of the Mississippi River in South Louisiana. The way the river bows through it has inspired one of New Orleans' nicknames, the Crescent City. Lake Pontchartrain sits to the north. The Gulf of Mexico lies to the west and south.

Its location has long made New Orleans a vital port. Port cities are typically lively places where people from different cultures mingle, and New Orleans is no exception. The city has also seen the flags of three different countries fly over it: Spain, France, and the United States. Its French heritage has remained particularly strong. The cultures of the Caribbean have had an influence as well. All of this has created a rich gumbo of culture. (Gumbo is a popular stew of South Louisiana.)

THE LIFESTYLE

New Orleans is a predominantly Catholic city. This sets it apart from the rest of the South, where Protestantism is prevalent. We see the influence of Catholicism in such News Orleans events as Mardi Gras. This boisterous carnival has taken place each year just before Lent since the 18th century. For a week, Mardi Gras seems to consume the entire city.

Mardi Gras reflects a festive attitude towards life. It is a New Orleans hallmark. The parade that caps Mardi Gras each year echoes something more. The city has an age-old love of proces-

19th century Mardi Gras scene

sion. Parades for weddings, funerals, Catholic feast days, and other occasions have enriched New Orleans life since at least the early 19th century.

New Orleans is also famous for its relaxed, carefree lifestyle. It partly comes from the hard living that its residents have historically had to endure. Survival and therefore life are to be celebrated. The attitude has led to two other nicknames for New Orleans: the City that Care Forgot and the Big Easy.

Before the Civil War, almost all African-Americans in the South were enslaved. New Orleans was different. It enjoyed a sizable free black population, which allowed black culture to develop more freely in the city. African roots could also be embraced more openly.

There was slavery in New Orleans. However, things were again different than elsewhere in the South. For one thing, New Orleans slaves could freely gather on Sundays in an open field known as Congo Square. There they sang, danced, and played instruments. The music filling the square sounded African and eventually mixed with styles from the Caribbean.

THE CREOLE POPULATION

Antebellum (before the Civil War) New Orleans also had a flourishing Creole population. It was made up of people having mixed European and African ancestry. Some Creole had Native American blood, too. The group identified closely with its European heritage.

Many Creole in New Orleans led prosperous lives before the Civil War. The community included business owners, doctors, lawyers, teachers, and newspaper publishers. Some even owned slaves, and one Creole manufacturer employed over 200 workers. Quite a few members of the community did well enough to send their children to France for schooling.

Creole prosperity promoted a vibrant cultural existence. This was especially true when it came to music. Classically trained Creole musicians performed professionally and gave lessons. There was even a Creole opera house and symphony orchestra. This was New Orleans after all, the most musical place in the country before the Civil War. One visitor called the city "one vast waltzing and gallopating hall."

The people of New Orleans have long enjoyed parades as well. The love of music and procession came together in an antebellum flowering of brass bands. In 1838, a local newspaper observed, "There is a mania in this city for horn and trumpet playing." Each of the main ethnic groups had its own bands. They would play for parades as well as dances, public picnics, and even funeral processions.

New Orleans continued to bask in the richness of its diverse cultural heritage for some years after the Civil War. However, things began to change with reestablishment of white authority from the late 1870s. As Jim Crow laws became the norm across the South, the Creole and black populations of New Orleans found themselves deprived of more and more rights. They also suffered a decrease in social status.

The Creole population of New Orleans felt this disenfranchisement most severely. Before the Civil War, it considered itself separate from and superior to the city's black citizens. Jim Crow laws though made little distinction between degrees of blackness. Any African ancestry made one black.

By the end of the 19th century, the status of New Orleans' Creoles had largely evaporated. They found themselves lumped together with the city's black population as a single ethnic group. The two came to share the same poverty and injustice.

THE ARRIVAL OF FREEDMEN

In the decades after the Civil War, New Orleans also saw an influx of freed slaves from other parts of the South. Emancipation had brought former slaves mobility. Many did not stray far from the plantations where they had once toiled. Others took the opportunity to relocate. New Orleans was a popular destination for freedmen, and it swelled the

SUGGESTED LISTENING

JELLY ROLL MORTON
"Black Bottom Stomp"
"Jelly Roll Blues"

KID ORY
"Gut Bucket Blues"
"Muskrat Ramble"

KING OLIVER
"Dipper Mouth Blues"
"King Porter Stomp"
"St. James Infirmary"

THE ORIGINAL DIXIELAND JAZZ BAND
"Darktown Strutters' Ball"
"Tiger Rag"

city's black population.

Freed slaves brought with them to New Orleans the type of music making they had developed on Southern plantations. Spirituals, work songs, infant forms of the blues, and even rural band traditions all found their way to New Orleans. (We learned about a number of these traditions in Chapter 1.) What had already been a city alive with music became even livelier.

The Birth of Jazz

Almost everything important in music came from him. —LOUIS ARMSTRONG ON KING OLIVER

A number of cultural and musical strands started coming together in New Orleans towards the end of the 19th century. As they did, they helped give birth to jazz.

Two of the strands were a marriage of the New Orleans brass band tradition and a musical fad that had swept America. During the last decades of the 19th century, military ensembles and the marches they played enjoyed widespread popularity. Bandmasters like John Phillip Sousa and Patrick Gilmore set American feet tapping across the country. Sousa was in fact one of the best-known musicians in the country at the turn of the 20th century.

New Orleans brass bands of the time capitalized on the popularity of marching music. The most prominent ensembles included the Excelsior Brass Band and Onward Brass Band, both featuring accomplished Creole musicians. Their popularity came in part from the inclusion of military marches during performances at picnics, fish fries, political rallies, and other events. At the same time, they were absorbing another musical influence.

It is said that the schooled Creole musicians of New Orleans at first dismissed the music brought to the city by rural freedmen. They supposedly found it raw and unsophisticated. Still, they must have been impressed by its syncopation and soulfulness. At any rate, what had been separate musical traditions started coming together as Creole culture collapsed into the city's black population.

Just as this blending of Creole and black styles was taking place, a new type of music found its way to New Orleans. Rags were the novel musical concoction we learned about in the previous chapter. Their march-like strains and heavy doses of syncopation spread down the Mississippi from the Midwest. By the 1890s, brass bands in New Orleans had taken them up.

In the same decade, the City of New Orleans created the pleasure district known as Storyville. The idea was to limit gambling, drinking, and other forms of adult entertainment to one part of town. It worked and Storyville quickly prospered and grew. This provided steady employment for brass bands at saloons and dance halls in the district. It also presented a wonderful incubator for the birth of jazz.

LIVES AND TIMES

Storyville New Orleans alderman Sidney Story drew up plans to limit red-light businesses to one section of the city. He was likely not pleased that it came to bear his name after its opening, in 1897. Storyville provided steady performance opportunities for the musicians that developed the original form of jazz. Many of them moved elsewhere, especially to Chicago, upon the district's closing, in 1917.

Prohibition Three years after the close of Storyville, the Eighteenth Amendment to the United States Constitution made the selling and drinking of alcohol illegal. This forced alcohol-servicing clubs to go underground. They became known as speakeasies and served as venues for live jazz through the 1920s. Prohibition was repealed in 1933.

Plessy v. Ferguson A U.S. Supreme Court decision that affirmed a Louisiana state law that mandated segregation. It contributed to a merging of New Orleans' Creole and black cultures. In turn, this created conditions that helped give birth to traditional jazz.

Just a couple of years after the founding of Storyville, ragtime music swept the nation. People everywhere were suddenly bobbing their heads to the syncopated strains of Scott Joplin's "Maple Leaf Rag." Pianists and brass bands across the country joined in to seize the moment. The popularity of ragtime was of course good news for the rag-playing brass bands of Storyville.

BUDDY BOLDEN AND HIS SUCCESSORS

One early Storyville band musician stood out above the rest. Cornet master Buddy Bolden (1877–1931) had a musical style all his own. His playing was powerful, loose, and soulful, and he made an art of improvising around melodies. He also mixed blues with ragtime and brought to this new blend the feel of black American church music.

The ensemble Buddy Bolden led set the standard for early jazz

Buddy Bolden

bands. The front row was like a miniature marching band—one each of cornet, trombone, and clarinet. Banjo or guitar, string bass, and drums provided rhythm and harmony behind these wind instruments.

Bolden's reign in Storyville did not last long, but soon other New Orleans musicians were developing the musical approach he forged. One of the most prominent was another cornet player and bandleader Joe "King" Oliver (1885–1938). As Louis Armstrong (1901–1971), who would become the most famous of New Orleans jazz artists, put it several decades later, "If it had not been for Joe Oliver, jazz would not be what it is today."

Collective improvisation emerged as key to King Oliver's music and that of other Storyville musicians. The cornet in a band would play the melody of a piece, leaving the trombone and clarinet free to weave musical lines around it. As the approach developed, improvised solos by individual band members also became common. With this practice the music ceased being ragtime. It became jazz.

Other talented individuals helped give birth to jazz in the first two decades of the 20th century. They included trombonist Edward "Kid" Ory, clarinetist Johnny Dodds, saxophonist Sidney Bechet, and cornetist "Bunk" Johnson. As these musicians began to tour, they also spread jazz beyond New Orleans.

Creole pianist and composer Jelly Roll Morton played a large role in this process. A relentless self-promoter, Morton even claimed that he had personally invented jazz. While not true, he was the first great jazz pianist. He also showed the world that the music could be successfully arranged and notated.

OUTSIDE OF NEW ORLEANS

Chicago and New York were two of the first cities outside of New Orleans to welcome jazz with open arms. In 1915, trombonist Tom Brown brought his ensemble, Band from Dixieland, to Chicago for four months and then to New York for a similar length of time. The success of Brown's band not only helped popularize jazz beyond Storyville, it lent jazz a name that some

New Orleans musicians did not particularly like, Dixieland.

Another New Orleans group followed in the footsteps of the Band from Dixieland. The Original Dixieland Jazz Band found their way to Chicago in 1916. By 1917, they were making a stir in New York City. The band became even more successful with the release of "Livery Stable Blues." The first jazz record ever publicly released, it was a smash hit and may have sold as many as a million copies.

Other jazz bands were soon heard on vinyl. Jazz was enjoying white-hot popularity similar to that of ragtime after the release of "Maple Leaf Rag." There were a few wrinkles, though.

THE QUESTION OF AUTHENTICITY

The Original Dixieland Jazz Band also claimed to have invented jazz. It had not. What the group instead accomplished was popularizing a somewhat watered-down imitation of the real thing. The band also turned some of the colorful playing techniques used by Storyville musicians into clichéd novelties.

All of this established a pattern in the history of jazz. The Original Dixieland Jazz Band enjoyed widespread popularity performing music developed primarily within the black community. Some would call this expropriation—taking something away from another for your own use.

The success of the Original Dixieland Jazz Band did bring some recognition to black artists. However, it also undercut the music's authenticity. The same phenomenon has played out time and again in jazz and beyond. Popular rapper Eminem even admits to it in "Without Me" when he raps, "I am the worst thing since Elvis Presley to do black music so selfishly."

DIPPERMOUTH BLUES

It would take a few years for more authentic New Orleans jazz to appear on record. One landmark recording came in 1923 with "Dippermouth Blues" by King Oliver and his Creole Jazz Band. An original work by Oliver, many other jazz musicians would go on to perform it down through the years.

The recording features Oliver on lead cornet and Johnny Dodds on clarinet. The band also includes trombone in the front line and a rhythm section of piano, banjo, and drums. You also hear a second cornet intertwined with Oliver. It is played by a young Louis Armstrong, whom you'll learn much more about in the next chapter.

After a short introductory line played by the entire group, the band lets loose with two rollicking 12-bar blues choruses. (A chorus is a main, repeated section of a musical work.) Oliver and Armstrong carry the melody while the clarinet flits merrily above them. The trombone improvises a more sustained countermelody underneath. This is an example of collective New Orleans improvisation at its finest.

After the band has dispensed with the melody, Dodds improvises two choruses filled with the sort of scooping, wailing long notes, and fast vibrato that are the essence of New Orleans clarinet playing. Meanwhile, everyone else repeats a punctuated, three-note phrase that leaves beat 4 of each measure empty.

After Dodds's solo, the band returns for another chorus of collective improvisation. Three improvised choruses by Oliver follow — one of the most famous solos in early jazz. In fact, Benny Goodman's band included the solo, note-for-note, when it rerecorded "Dippermouth Blues" a decade later.

Oliver uses a plunger during the solo as a mute to make his

cornet "talk." He was known for this wah-wah technique as well as his bluesy playing. When you listen, you hear that his solo is made up of repeated phrases and a limited range of notes. Despite this—or maybe because of it—a lot of soul pours from Oliver's horn. It is easy to understand why this solo became so influential.

Preservation Hall Jazz Band

At the end of Oliver's solo, everyone stops for a few beats while the drummer shouts out, "Oh, play that thing!" This propels the band into one last chorus of group improvisation, and a short, catchy rhythmic phrase punctuates the end of the recording.

Oliver and his Creole Jazz Band actually recorded "Dippermouth Blues" in Indiana rather than New Orleans, as Oliver moved to Chicago in 1919. Historical developments often result from both push and pull factors. Oliver's migration serves as a good example.

The pull for Oliver and other jazz musicians was the popularity jazz had experienced in Chicago. It started when Tom Brown brought the music there a few years earlier. An important push was the closing of Storyville in 1917. With it went opportunities for New Orleans musicians in their hometown.

Oliver first played in a Chicago band led by Bill Johnson. By 1922, though, he was heading up his own group in the city. He soon surrounded himself with some of his favorite musicians from New Orleans, most notably Johnny Dodds and Louis Armstrong. For a brief moment in time, they made up the hottest band in Chicago.

THE ROARING TWENTIES

The 1920s were known as the Roaring Twenties. It was a prosperous, dynamic decade, full of exuberance in big cities like Chicago and New York. Americans developed a huge appetite for modern life and its trappings, including automobiles, moving pictures, and speakeasies (illegal nightclubs).

Jazz could be found in more and more cities across the country as the 1920s progressed. It made the perfect soundtrack for a thoroughly modern era. A new technology of that decade, radio, helped it spread. Jazz even became popular overseas as musicians began touring internationally. The immense popularity of jazz led to another nickname for the 1920s, the Jazz Age.

By 1930, jazz had started to grow beyond the traditional style first heard in New Orleans. As we'll see in our next chapter, Louis Armstrong was most responsible for this development. In particular, he served as an important musical bridge to the next big thing in jazz, swing.

As new jazz styles developed, the music of New Orleans jazz started sounding traditional. Artists have come along now and again to try and update it in various ways. For the most part, though, it is now treated as a living tradition. That is how you can still hear it at New Orleans' Preservation Hall. Since the 1960s, the venue has helped keep alive the music that first blossomed in Storyville a century ago.

With the passing of time, respect for the first generation of jazz musicians grew. There were various attempts to feature those still living as veteran artists of a bygone era. Trombonist "Kid" Ory was one such New Orleans artist to enjoy a comeback as a revered senior. The Library of Congress also recognized the importance of Jelly Roll Morton when it recorded a series of interviews and solo performances with him in 1938.

The Legacy of Traditional Jazz

Almost all of us have heard traditional jazz at one time or another. Just mention the song "When the Saints Go Marching In," and the sounds of Storyville fill our mind's ear. Most of us call it Dixieland but recognize that it originated in New Orleans. Indeed, the music continues to draw many tourists to the Crescent City.

There would be no jazz if not for the music that developed in New Orleans, especially in Storyville, in the early decades of the 20th century. In that sense, traditional jazz enjoys the most important legacy of all. It is the fount from which all other forms have developed.

The early jazz of New Orleans established the tradition of improvisation that is still at the heart of the music. It also set the model in terms of instrumentation. To this day, jazz bands tend to feature a rhythm section fronted by such wind instruments as trumpet, trombone, and saxophone.

The original vitality of early jazz can still be heard in New Orleans. You sense it in the modern-day brass bands that continue to perform in parades, for social clubs, and on street corners. The music of a Dirty Dozen Brass Band may be quite different from that of King Oliver. But listen past the funk and bebop influences, and you can still hear the heartbeat of Storyville jazz in its rollicking spontaneity.

Louis Armstrong

SATCHMO!
LOUIS ARMSTRONG

Armstrong is to music what Einstein is to physics and the Wright Brothers are to travel.
—KEN BURNS

Television viewers in the 1960s knew Louis Armstrong as a grandfatherly entertainer with a deep, gravelly voice. Pops made famous songs like "Mack the Knife" and "Hello, Dolly!" while flashing an ear-to-ear smile for the camera. A charming performer, he would clutch a white handkerchief and exclaim, "Oh, yeah!" at the end of songs. While he often held a trumpet, he didn't play it as much as he sang.

The young Louis Armstrong was quite different. In the 1920s and 1930s, Armstrong reigned as the hottest of the hot young jazz artists. He blew the trumpet with such brilliance that he could have brought down the walls of Jericho. He also blazed a trail as a pioneer of jazz improvisation and helped take jazz from New Orleans to Chicago and far beyond. It made him one of America's most respected musicians and a celebrated figure around the world.

Early Life

He was born poor, died rich, and never hurt anyone along the way. —DUKE ELLINGTON

Louis Armstrong believed he was born on July 4, 1900. He was very proud of the date. It suggested that he was a true child of America born at the dawn of a new century, just like jazz. (After his death, researchers discovered that he was actually born on July 6, 1901.) Armstrong and jazz also share the same birthplace. While jazz was developing in the Storyville section of New Orleans, he was growing up over in a poor area of the city known as Back of Town.

The grandson of slaves, Armstrong had a difficult childhood. His father abandoned him when he was still a baby, and his mother was absent from time to time, too. His grandmother helped watch out for him, but poverty and an unstable home life marked Armstrong' early years. He wrote about this time in his autobiography, "I lived with my mother in Jane's Alley in a place called Brick Row—a lot of cement, rented rooms sort of like a motel."

SCHOOL DAYS

Armstrong enrolled in the Fisk School for Boys near his home when he turned six. Fisk was a segregated school for black children that offered its students a rich musical experience. It put on operettas (light operas), boasted a fine choir, and employed respected music teachers from the Creole community. While he apparently wasn't the best of students and even played hooky quite a bit, Armstrong learned to read and write at Fisk. He also took up the cornet, a close relative to the trumpet.

To make money as a boy, Armstrong sold newspapers, sang and danced on street corners, unloaded banana boats, and even collected discarded food to sell to restaurants. He also helped vend coal from a wagon that went street to street through Storyville. The police normally kept children out of that section of the city, but delivering coal granted Armstrong access. What he enjoyed most there was hearing the legendary Joe "King" Oliver playing trumpet with his band at a cabaret. Armstrong remembered, "He was blowing up a storm on trumpet. Nobody could touch him."

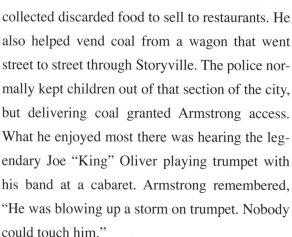

SUGGESTED LISTENING

LOUIS ARMSTRONG AND THE HOT 5
"Heebie Jeebies"
"West End Blues"

AS SOLO ARTIST
"Up a Lazy River"
"Stardust"
"Hello, Dolly!"
"Mack the Knife"
"What a Wonderful World"

Oliver was a great inspiration to Armstrong. "It was my ambition to play as he did." He also gave the younger musician one of his old cornets and served as a mentor. "I can never stop loving Joe Oliver. He was always ready to come to my rescue when I needed someone to tell me about life and its intricate little things and helped me out of difficult situations."

Armstrong was apparently in these difficult situations quite often as he grew up. He dropped out of Fisk's when he was 11 and wound up being sent to a New Orleans home for waifs (neglected or abandoned children) on a number of occasions. Once it was for firing a pistol into the air on New Year's Eve. At the waif's home, a professor named Peter Davis taught Louis a great deal about playing the trumpet. Eventually, Davis made his student the leader of the home's brass band.

PARADE BANDS

When he was 14, Armstrong was released from the waif's home and started playing in New Orleans brass band parades. He did all he could to listen to and learn from the city's earliest jazz musicians, including the legendary Buddy Bolden. Soon, Armstrong found himself touring with the band of Fate Marable. The group played on riverboats plying the Mississippi River. Armstrong called performing with Marable "going to the university," because he learned so much from it.

In 1919, Armstrong got his first big break as a musician. King Oliver decided to move north to Chicago, and Armstrong took his mentor's place in the Kid Ory band. The group had the reputation of being the hottest jazz band in New Orleans. It became even hotter with Armstrong. They played funerals, parades, society dances at the country club, and a variety of other venues. Between gigs with Ory, Armstrong continued to deliver coal and play with other bands.

Armstrong developed quickly as a musician and was soon being featured on extended improvisations. This made him one of the first jazz soloists to enjoy the spotlight in this way. He took advantage of the opportunity. Perhaps more than any other early jazz musician, Armstrong developed the art of improvisation. He started to solo in a way that would inspire many other musicians.

CHICAGO

In 1922, King Oliver invited Armstrong to join his Chicago ensemble, the Creole Jazz Band. This group enjoyed the reputation of being the best jazz band there, and its success allowed Armstrong to become a full-time musician. It gave him a chance to

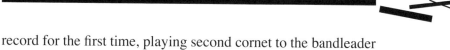

record for the first time, playing second cornet to the bandleader on sessions for the Gennett and Okeh labels. Armstrong also met his second wife, Lil Hardin, while playing in the Oliver band. She was the group's pianist.

Armstrong quickly established a musical reputation in Chicago. He began his career there by improvising backing parts behind Oliver's lead playing, but he was a bolder player than his mentor. Oliver tended to blend in with the band while Armstrong became more inventive and virtuosic. As this happened, Hardin encouraged Armstrong to step forward as a solo artist.

Armstrong started showing a remarkable ability for playing high notes while he was with Oliver's band. (He is said to have once played 200 high C notes in a row.) However, he would eventually pay a price for this flair. The physical pressure of playing too high too long on a brass instrument permanently deformed his lips. In turn, this inspired one of his nicknames, Satchelmouth, eventually shortened to Satchmo.

The Hot Five and Hot Seven

He became the beacon, the light in the tower that helped the rest of us navigate the tricky waters of jazz improvisation.—ELLIS MARSALIS

Armstrong left King Oliver's band in 1924 and soon joined the Fletcher Henderson Orchestra in New York City. Henderson led one of the most famous jazz ensembles of the day, and Armstrong switched from cornet to trumpet to fit in better. He had to adapt his style of playing somewhat, too. Henderson's brand of jazz was more controlled than what Armstrong had played in New Orleans or Chicago. He also started singing with the group.

On the side, Armstrong recorded with a number of famous blues singers of that era.

Just over a year later, Armstrong returned to Chicago and started playing with a number of bands. He recorded under his name for the first time towards the end of 1925. This marked the beginning of a series of recordings for the Okeh label that continued until 1928. They feature fellow musicians from New Orleans who played with Armstrong in Oliver's Chicago band.

Louis Armstrong's Hot Five and Hot Seven groups included such Louisiana veterans as Johnny Dodds on clarinet and Kid Ory on trombone. The group never performed lived. Still, its recordings stand as jazz masterpieces.

WEST END BLUES

One of the Hot Five's final and best recordings is of King Oliver's "West End Blues" (1928). The laidback performance begins with Armstrong improvising a marvelous unaccompanied *cadenza* on cornet. A cadenza is an unaccompanied passage by

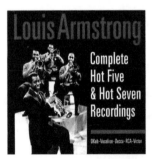

a soloist that is typically quite acrobatic. It allows the solo performer a moment alone in the spotlight to fully show off. A cadenza also usually has no steady beat.

Armstrong's "West End Blues" cadenza introduction bobs and weaves as it makes it way up to and then back down from a soaring high C. Its flexible beat dances with syncopation. Stylistically, it was years ahead of its time.

"West End Blues" is a traditional 12-bar blues. However, there is something modern-sounding about the way Armstrong plays the melody. It almost swings. Much of Armstrong's play-

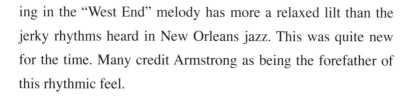

ing in the "West End" melody has more a relaxed lilt than the jerky rhythms heard in New Orleans jazz. This was quite new for the time. Many credit Armstrong as being the forefather of this rhythmic feel.

DEVELOPING THE MODERN STYLE

Armstrong's recording of "West End Blues" is quite far from New Orleans jazz in other ways. For example, the accompanying wind instruments don't play countermelodies. They instead hold out long notes that together create chords. Also, the famous jazz pianist Earl "Fatha" Hines simply *comps* on each downbeat.

Comping, an abbreviation of accompanying, is a chordal rather than melodic style of background playing. By comping on the downbeats throughout "West End Blues," Hines provides a firm harmonic foundation for the song. He also stays out of the way of each soloist. Comping is an approach used by all modern jazz pianists.

Hines continues to comp with his left hand during his own solo. However, his right makes up for lack of activity earlier in the song. He twists and turns through a series of fast, tinkling single-note runs. This makes his solo also sound years ahead of its time.

At the beginning of the last chorus, Armstrong displays his lung capacity by holding a high B♭ for four long measures. He fills out the next four bars with one of the most famous jazz phrases of all time. It is superbly inventive and technically brilliant yet also wonderfully soulful. In just four bars, Armstrong proves exactly how masterful of a musician he could be.

If all of that wasn't enough magic for one song, "West End Blues" also includes a delightfully relaxed example of Armstrong's *scat* singing—vocal improvisation that relies on word-less syllables. (He can also be heard scatting a couple of years earlier on the Hot Five recording of "Heebie Jeebies.") Armstrong became so closely associated with this type of singing that many think he invented it. Whether he did or not, his recordings certainly show that he was its first true master.

Finding His Voice

Armstrong moved back to New York in 1929 after breaking up with Lil Hardin. He played in the pit orchestra for the successful musical *Hot Chocolate* and at the popular Harlem nightclub Connie's Inn—an important section of Manhattan we'll learn more about in later chapters. He also started to turn away from playing the cornet or trumpet some in favor of singing.

Singing was nothing new for Armstrong. He had done so as a child on the streets of New Orleans and with Fletcher Henderson's orchestra. In the 1930s, though, he came to rely on singing as much as playing trumpet or cornet.

A relatively new invention helped inspire Armstrong's switch to vocalizing. Until the mid-1920s, musicians had to perform loudly into a large funnel to record. Microphones changed all of that. In particular, the ribbon microphone made it possible to record the subtleties of even the softest sounds. Pair a microphone with an amplifier and a singer could also be as loud as an entire band in live performance.

The microphone soon ushered in a new type of singer. Murmuring crooners began to take the place of bellowing singers with leather lungs. Instead of shouting lyrics the way a Bessie Smith or Al Jolson would in the 1920s, a crooner like Bing Crosby could softly sing them in a relaxed, romantic style.

The wide dynamic and expressive range of Armstrong's singing was ideal for this new age of the microphone. Make no mistake. Armstrong could shout with the best of them. But he also gently intoned many phrases, plus his singing was alive with an incredible range of nuance. Many singers use only a few vocal colors. Armstrong colored songs with an entire 64-crayon box!

Listen to Armstrong's 1931 recording of "Up a Lazy River" by the great American songwriter Hoagy Carmichael and you'll understand. His singing is relaxed and understated on many phrases. He also sings for most of the recording and only picks up the trumpet in the last section. Even so, he still seems to be thinking like an instrumentalist throughout the song. You can hear it in the way he phrases the melody when he first starts singing and in the scat improvisation that follows.

IN THE SWING OF THINGS

The 1930s came to be known as the swing era, and almost the entire performance of "Up a Lazy River" announces the arrival of this new form of jazz. It's there in the sophisticated arrangement, the melodic phrasing, the rhythmic style, and the tempo.

With "West End Blues," you can mainly hear it in Armstrong's playing. Now, the entire ensemble swings—except maybe for the saxophones at the beginning of the song. Bing Crosby called Armstrong the "Master of Swing," and we can certainly hear why in "Up a Lazy River."

Singers like Crosby not only praised Armstrong, many were highly influenced by him. From crooners like Crosby to "scatifying" jazz stylists like Ella Fitzgerald, a wide array of popular vocalists found inspiration in Armstrong's innovations.

The 1930s are remembered as the swing era. But they were

also defined by the Great Depression, in which the entire country struggled economically, jazz musicians included. Even many of the most established jazz artists floundered and turned to work in other fields. Seeking new opportunities, Armstrong migrated west to Los Angeles in 1930. He found some success performing live, playing on radio broadcasts, and even appearing in the movie *Ex-Flame*.

Armstrong didn't stay long in Los Angeles, though. By 1931, he was back in Chicago and then soon after returned to New Orleans. His hometown gave the onetime waif the type of welcome reserved for returning heroes. Again, the stay didn't last long. Armstrong soon struck out on a performance tour of the country and then headed for Europe.

For the rest of his life, Armstrong spent much of his time touring. Some years, he performed over 300 gigs. The Queens borough of New York City served as home when he wasn't on the road. The band backing Armstrong when he performed was known as the "All Stars" and featured a number of well-known jazz artists, including trombonist Jack Teagarden and Earl "Fatha" Hines—the pianist who recorded with the Hot Five.

Armstrong sang more and played trumpet less as the years went by. Too many high notes over time just made it too dif-

LIVES AND TIMES

Roaring Twenties This is the nickname given to the 1920s. It reflects the carefree, exuberant lifestyle found in big cities like New York and Chicago during that decade. In this time of economic prosperity after the upheaval of World War I, many Americans turned to the enjoyment provided by modern technologies. They toured around in automobiles, went to see movies in theatres, and listened to recordings of hot jazz on mechanical record players. Jazz became so popular during the 1920s that the decade is also known as the Jazz Age.

Great Depression The stock market crash of 1929 marked the end of the Roaring Twenties. Soon banks across the country failed and many Americans lost their jobs. Throughout the 1930s, the United States economy struggled, causing prolonged hardship for many people. The cheerful dance music known as swing helped the country forget about its problems to a certain extent.

American Civil Rights Movement In the 1950s, Black Americans began to formally protest the racial inequality they endured almost a century after gaining freedom from slavery. Individual activists like Rosa Parks defied the injustice of segregation while national leaders like Dr. Martin Luther King Jr. held rallies for equal treatment under the law. The movement led to the passage of the Civil Rights Act of 1964 and the 1965 Voting Rights Act.

ficult for him to play his instrument much. As a result, he started reserving the trumpet for studio sessions and cameo appearances during live performances.

NATIONAL TREASURE

In the 1940s, Armstrong began to emerge as a celebrity. He appeared in dozens of movies, typically performing music as himself and displaying his bubbly personality. He even appeared on the cover of *Time* magazine in 1949, the first jazz musician to be so honored. His fame spread and he eventually became well known around the world, enjoying audiences with the crowned heads of Europe and Pope Paul VI.

Around the same time, America's State Department began sponsoring overseas tours of Armstrong and his band. "Ambassador Satch" played jazz and spread goodwill across the globe. A 1956 concert in the African country of Ghana drew 100,000 listeners.

As a black American, Armstrong experienced prejudice throughout his career. Some thought he tried too hard to appeal to white audiences. While he may not have shown it much in public, Armstrong did support the American civil rights movement of the 1950s and 1960s in other ways. For one, he made significant financial contributions to Dr. Martin Luther King Jr. and others leading the fight for racial justice.

Pops, as he came to be widely known, occasionally spoke out against inequality. He famously condemned the violence accompanying the desegregation of Little Rock, Arkansas schools in 1957. He said publicly, "Do you dig me when I say I have a right to blow my top over injustice?" He even cancelled a planned overseas State Department tour in protest.

Armstrong scored the biggest hit of his career in 1964 when his recording of the Broadway song "Hello, Dolly!" reached #1 on the pop charts. It knocked the Beatles from the spot and made Armstrong the most senior chart-topper of all time at the ripe old age of 63.

Armstrong continued to perform and even tour until his death in 1971 from heart problems. In refusing to cancel a performance just months before he died, he said, "My whole life, my whole soul, my whole spirit is to blow that horn."

The news of Armstrong's passing made the front page of newspapers around the world. A host of celebrities attended his funeral, and a number of jazz greats carried his casket during the ceremony. They included Count Basie, Dizzy Gillespie, Duke Ellington, and Ella Fitzgerald.

Louis' Legacy

More has been written about Louis Armstrong's legacy than that of nearly every other jazz musician. Some commentators have emphasized his musical influence. Miles Davis, another trumpet luminary, said, "You can't play anything on a horn that Armstrong hasn't played." The *Oxford Companion to Jazz* states, "Not a single musician who has mastered that language [jazz] fails to make daily use, knowingly or unknowingly, of something that was invented by Louis Armstrong."

Armstrong's legacy goes far beyond notes on a horn and musical style. It extends to something soulful. Famed gospel singer Mahalia Jackson said, "If you don't like Louis Armstrong, you don't know how to love." The celebrated American composer Leonard Bernstein put it this way, "What he does is real, and true, and honest, and simple, and even noble. Every time this

man puts his trumpet to his lips, even if only to practice three notes, he does it with his whole soul."

But even this doesn't totally capture the legacy of Louis Armstrong. His personality and verve inspired many. South African trumpet master Hugh Masekela has said, "I think that Louis Armstrong loosened the world, helped people to be able to say 'Yeah,' and to walk with a little dip in their hip." Armstrong also served something deeper. Today's trumpet great Wynton Marsalis has said, "He left an undying testimony to the human condition."

Given all of this, is it any wonder that famous singer Tony Bennett remembers Louis Armstrong in the following way? "The bottom line of any country in the world is what did we contribute to the world. We contributed Louis Armstrong."

What did Armstrong have to say about himself? "What we play is life." That is both the simplest and perhaps the best tribute of all.

Benny Goodman

SWING

Ah, swing, well, we used to call it ragtime,
then blues—then jazz. Now, it's swing.
—LOUIS ARMSTRONG

In the 1930s, a new form of jazz gained popularity over New Orleans Dixieland and its Chicago offshoot. Swing favored big bands over small ensembles. A new instrument also came into the spotlight: the saxophone. These developments went hand in hand with a stylistic change. Swing had a looser rhythmic feel than New Orleans or Chicago jazz. This became the music's defining characteristic.

Swing relied less on improvisation as well. In traditional jazz, just about everyone improvised. With swing, soloing became the role of a few specialists within a band. Ensembles also started playing from written arrangements referred to as charts.

A younger generation of jazz musicians became popular during the swing era. Many were white, as opposed to the black musicians who first developed jazz in New Orleans. Swing artists like Benny Goodman and Glenn Miller helped broaden the popularity of jazz past America's lines of racial segregation.

The Roots of Swing

Playing with that band was the acid test. If you could make it with Fletcher, you could play with anybody. —BENNY CARTER

Hot jazz bands, like the one led by King Oliver, burned down the speakeasies of 1920s Chicago with their sizzling music. Meanwhile, a less intense style filled the society ballrooms of New York. There, Paul Whiteman, known as the "King of Jazz," reigned supreme. While smaller groups largely improvised jazz in Chicago, Whiteman's larger orchestra used tight, written arrangements.

Some historians question whether most of Whiteman's music was actually jazz. It may be better to call it jazz-influenced dance music. Even so, Whiteman did much to popularize jazz-style music among white Americans. He also helped bring an air of legitimacy to jazz by merging it with symphonic music. For example, Whiteman commissioned and debuted George Gershwin's "Rhapsody in Blue" in 1924.

Whiteman's orchestra employed white musicians only. This was standard in the segregated America of that time. A number of the players Whiteman relied on would go on to become well-known artists. They included trumpeter Bix Beiderbecke and trombonist Jack Teagarden.

In the 1920s, up in Harlem, another sort of jazz enjoyed much popularity. Fletcher Henderson's music was hotter than Whiteman's but more arranged than Chicago jazz. In fact, Henderson served as something of a bridge between these two worlds. New Orleans and Chicago trumpet legend Louis Armstrong played in Henderson's band for a while during 1924. Henderson also served as an arranger for Paul Whiteman.

Like Whiteman, Henderson relied on musicians who would go on to become famous in their own right. Don Redman and Coleman Hawkins became two of the best known. Both played saxophone. Such accomplished musicians helped establish their instrument as a central element in jazz. As we'll see in later chapters, the saxophone would become perhaps the most important of all lead instruments.

THE ARRIVAL OF THE BIG BAND

Both Whiteman's and Henderson's stars started to fade in the early 1930s. Their legacies continued, though. Together, they created a model for an orchestral type of jazz. It combined saxophones with trumpets and trombones as the main melodic instruments. This would become the standard during the 1930s. With a full-blown big band (large swing ensemble) of the late 1930s, you might find five saxophones and four each of trumpet and trombone.

This instrumentation is quite far from the small combos heard in early New Orleans jazz. Even the Chicago bands of King Oliver and Louis Armstrong included only one or two trumpets and a trombone. Chicago ensembles also relied more on the clarinet than the saxophone.

The New York and Chicago jazz bands of the 1920s were

alike in one important way. They featured the same sort of instruments to provide their rhythmic and harmonic foundation. In both, the rhythm section usually had as its core a set of drums and a piano and perhaps a tuba to play bass notes and a banjo to strum chords.

Swing band rhythm sections developed from this earlier model. The drum set and piano remained, but the tuba disappeared, replaced with the string bass and a new way of playing. Called walking bass, it relied on streams of one-beat notes that smoothly walked up and down musical scales. Swing also had little use for the banjo; in some bands, an acoustic guitar instead played a crisp chord on each downbeat.

LIVES AND TIMES

Great Depression A severe economic depression gripped America throughout the 1930s. Unemployment soared to 25%. To counteract its effect, President Franklin D. Roosevelt instituted the New Deal, a series of economic programs.

Joe Louis Known as the Brown Bomber, boxer Joe Louis mesmerized fight fans as he felled a string of opponents during his time as heavyweight champion, from 1937 to 1949. His honesty and work ethic made him a hero to many. They also become a symbol of America in his bouts against Germany's Max Schmeling.

World War II Nazi Germany's invasion of Poland in 1939 led to a military conflict that eventually embroiled most countries in the world. America entered the war after the bombing of Pearl Harbor, in 1941. Conflict ended with the surrender of the axis countries, Italy, Germany, and Japan, in 1945.

Golden Age of Radio Improved technology and national networks of stations made radio a key entertainment medium in the 1930s. Families across the country tuned in to hear radio series like "The Lone Ranger" and "The Green Hornet," boxing matches, breaking news bulletins, and live performances by famous musicians.

IN FULL SWING

As we saw in Chapter 3, Louis Armstrong exerted an important stylistic influence on the birth of swing music. Traditional New Orleans jazz featured a choppy, "ricky ticky" subdivision of the beat. Armstrong started to break from this rhythm in the late 1920s with his own trumpet playing.

Satchmo divided the beat in a smoother, more flowing way. You can hear it in the 1928 recording he made with his Hot Five of "West End Blues." By 1931, on his recording of "Up the Lazy River," the entire ensemble had joined in swinging with him.

Something else happened rhythmically. Dixieland pieces tended to be in 2/4 time, two beats per measure. This is a reflection of the style's ragtime and marching band heritage. Jazz in the 1930s started favoring 4/4, or four-beat measures. This rhythmic orientation was heard in many popular songs of the time.

TEXTURAL DEVELOPMENTS

A couple of final changes were taking place in jazz that helped give birth to swing. The written arrangements penned by Fletcher Henderson and others were less polyphonic (having simultaneous melodic lines) than what was heard in traditional jazz. To understand this, let's briefly review musical texture in Dixieland.

In the original New Orleans style of jazz, several lines of melody weave around one another at the same time. One instrument, typically the trumpet, carries the main melody. The other wind instruments, like the clarinet and trombone, improvise lines that complement this. It can get quite involved. It can even be hard to tell what is the main melody since the lead instrument will often improvise around it.

There is typically much more clarity in a swing arrangement. While some instruments might play countermelodies, there is usually no doubt about the main melody. It is played clearly and often in harmony by a number of instruments together. This is known as homophony.

The change from polyphony to homophony parallels a similar development in classical music almost two hundred years earlier. The music of the baroque period (1600–1750) was largely polyphonic. The greatest composers of the era, like Johann Sebastian Bach, excelled at writing polyphonic music.

A younger generation of composers turned away from polyphony during the classical period (1750–1820). Joseph Haydn and Wolfgang Amadeus Mozart instead favored the clarity of a single melody played by a number of instruments in harmony.

As written arrangements became the norm with jazz bands in the 1930s, the nature of improvisation changed. It permeated New Orleans and Chicago jazz. Almost all of the wind instruments improvised during the performance of a piece. With written swing charts, everyone started to play what was written on the page during the main part of an arrangement. Improvisation became the job of dedicated performers in an ensemble. They would stand to take solos in the middle of a piece.

The Birth of Swing

Benny Goodman has a style that can be identified before his name is announced.
—BEN POLLACK

The musician who most embodied the developing style of jazz that would blossom into swing was drummer Chick Webb. His orchestra began a historic run as the house band at the popular Savoy Ballroom in 1931. Located in Harlem, the Savoy became the epicenter of an early swing earthquake unleashed by Webb.

Webb's band swung and swung hard on original pieces like "Stompin' at the Savoy." Jazz musicians living in the city, both black and white, went up to Harlem to hear Webb. The musical pilgrims included Benny Goodman.

Goodman was a jazz clarinetist from Chicago who was enjoying a successful career as a studio musician in New York. During several months in early 1935, he performed on a national radio program, "Let's Dance." Webb inspired the music of the band

Goodman put together for the weekly show. (The swing arrangements Goodman's group played were by Fletcher Henderson.)

Goodman's live slot on "Let's Dance" was heard after midnight on the East Coast—when most people there were already asleep. However, the show came on midevening out West. Although he did not know it at the time, Goodman developed a sizable radio audience in California because of this.

Goodman set out on tour with his band across the country from New York in the summer of 1935. They met with little success at first and struggled financially. By the time they reached the Palomar Ballroom in Los Angeles for a three-week engagement, the band was disillusioned.

The group's first night at the Palomar did not begin well, either. The band had put away its Fletcher Henderson swing arrangements in favor of society dance music. The Palomar audience failed to respond. Frustrated, the group's drummer, Gene Krupa, said, "If we're gonna die, Benny, let's die playing our own thing."

At the beginning of its next set, the band let loose with a swing arrangement. The audience went wild. The Benny Goodman they knew from "Let's Dance" had arrived, and the swing era was born.

SUGGESTED LISTENING

CHICK WEBB
"Harlem Congo"
"Stompin' at the Savoy"

BENNY GOODMAN
"Avalon"
"King Porter Stomp"
"Let's Dance"
"Sing, Sing, Sing"

ARTIE SHAW
"Begin the Beguine"

GLENN MILLER
"In the Mood"
Tommy Dorsey
"Well, Git It!"

THE KING OF SWING

Goodman quickly became one of the most popular musicians in the country through more radio and live performances. He soon earned the title the King of Swing.

During a tour, Goodman heard a young percussionist named

Lionel Hampton and invited him to join his group. Hampton was a gifted player who popularized the *vibraphone*—an amplified metal-keyed relative of the marimba. He also happened to be African American, and at the time, popular music was highly

Lionel Hampton

segrated. Goodman's hiring of Hampton, guitarist Charlie Christian, and others helped break down such barriers.

In 1936, Goodman and his band returned to New York, where they enjoyed an extended engagement at the Hotel Pennsylvania's Manhattan Room. In March of the following year, Goodman and his orchestra played New York's Paramount Theater.

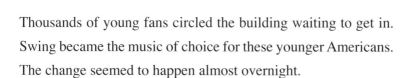

Thousands of young fans circled the building waiting to get in. Swing became the music of choice for these younger Americans. The change seemed to happen almost overnight.

Many older listeners did not like the style. It seemed like a corruption of the respectable society music played by Paul Whiteman. There were no strings to sweeten the sound, the tempos could be insanely fast, and there was too much improvisation.

These critics were not alone. Others thought that swing was doing terrible things to the music of black America. The famous blues pioneer W.C. Handy wrote in his autobiography, "Prominent white orchestra leaders, concert singers, and others are making commercial use of Negro music in its various phases. That's why they introduced swing, which is not a musical form."

Some outside of America also disapproved of swing. In particular, the Nazi regime that controlled Germany banned the music altogether. The Nazis did not like the music's connection with minorities in America and opposed the spread of the lifestyle that swing seemed to promote.

Something else about swing bothered some people but delighted many young folks both in America and abroad. It was great for dancing and inspired a number of dance crazes. The jitterbug was the most famous of these. More conservative people considered its movements wild and improper.

SING, SING, SING (WITH A SWING)

Benny Goodman ended the Paramount show with one of his most famous pieces. It was an instrumental version of a song by Louis Prima, "Sing, Sing, Sing (With a Swing)." The band recorded a studio version of the piece later in the year.

At that time, a phonograph record could only contain several minutes of music on each of its two sides. The Goodman recording of "Sing, Sing, Sing" is extraordinary in many ways. For one, it spills over Side A of the record to continue on Side B. Despite being in a fast 4/4 tempo, the performance clocks in at over eight and a half minutes long.

Gene Krupa

The Goodman arrangement begins with Gene Krupa hammering out a pulsating rhythm on his floor tom drum for eight measures. Trombones and low saxophones join in with a syncopated lick that is capped by growling trumpets. The melody then

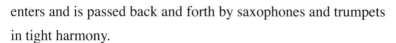

enters and is passed back and forth by saxophones and trumpets in tight harmony.

After the melody has been stated, Goodman begins a brief but smoldering improvisation on clarinet. Its swinging feel is very different from the type of clarinet playing heard in Dixieland. Krupa then returns with the throbbing floor tom beat heard at the beginning of the piece, and the band returns to the melody. For the rest of Side A on the original phonograph record, the wind instruments and Krupa trade hot phrases.

At the beginning of Side B, we hear a long, wailing tenor saxophone improvisation. Goodman briefly solos again. Then different groups of horns, including blaring trombones and growling trumpets, start playing repeating phrases. Together they form a harmonized polyphony that gives way to a brief Krupa drum solo.

Next comes a wonderful improvisation by the legendary trumpeter Harry James. The band helps James end the solo with a short musical tag. Goodman echoes the tag as the beginning of his own extended solo. It is accompanied only by Krupa, on floor tom. The clarinet improvisation eventually melts away into a few soft trills and a subdued solo by Krupa. He announces its end with a few beats on a cowbell, and the entire band enters to play a fiery ending.

SWING DEVELOPS

Other swing bands would soon become popular alongside Benny Goodman's. They included one led by fellow clarinetist Artie Shaw and the ensemble fronted by the brothers Tommy and Jimmy Dorsey. Each band had a somewhat different approach, but all shared a love of swing. Radio helped popularize big bands, bringing jazz out of the nightclubs and into America's living rooms.

Trombonist Glenn Miller had perhaps the most popular swing big band on the eve of America's entry into the World War II. Miller's Duke Ellington and Count Basie led bands of a different nature. We'll get to them in the next chapter.

Tommy Dorsey and singer Beryl Davis at New York's WMCA radio

Many swing bands featured solo singers, some of whom became quiet famous. Frank Sinatra first recorded professionally as a member of a band led by former Benny Goodman trumpeter Harry James. While Sinatra was more of a pop singer who was influenced by jazz, a number of out-and-out jazz singers also started with swing bands. Ella Fitzgerald, for example, began her career with the Chick Webb band.

Goodman's own star continued to shine during the remainder of the 1930s. In late 1937, he and his band trekked up to Harlem, where they competed against Webb's orchestra in the "Music Battle of the Century." It was held at the Savoy Ballroom, Webb's home turf.

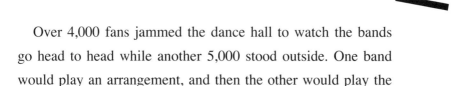

Over 4,000 fans jammed the dance hall to watch the bands go head to head while another 5,000 stood outside. One band would play an arrangement, and then the other would play the same thing. Both bands had exhausted themselves by the end. All agree that Webb won the friendly competition, which would go down in history as one of the most famous jazz performances of all time.

Less than a year later, Goodman and his band headlined another historic performance. New York City's Carnegie Hall was and remains the most important venue for classical music in the country. Goodman's appearance there in 1938 marked a new cultural arrival for jazz.

Jazz had started out as an obscure musical form by African-Americans in the city of New Orleans. With Goodman's appearance at Carnegie Hall, it had fully crossed the racial divide to become a celebrated music of an entire nation.

The Benny Goodman Carnegie Hall concert included a musical history of jazz and performances by members of the Count Basie and Duke Ellington bands. The climax came with a scorching hot performance by Goodman and his full band of "Sing, Sing, Sing." Gene Krupa's pounding floor tom introduction echoes in the rafters of Carnegie Hall to this day.

THE DEMISE OF SWING

Swing remained extremely popular into the early 1940s. It then suffered a rapid decline. By the end of World War II, in 1945, the swing era was largely over. What happened?

A number of factors contributed to swing's fall from popularity. For one, many swing musicians served in the military during the war and wound up overseas. Even for musicians still in

America, it became difficult to tour because of rations on gasoline and the rubber used in tires. Such factors led to small combos replacing big bands at dances across the country.

Swing also suffered a self-inflicted wound. The union representing most instrumentalists, the American Federation of Musicians, went on strike in 1942 against all of the major record companies. The walkout lasted for over a year. During that time, no instrumental music was recorded.

A number of record companies started recording singers like Frank Sinatra backed only by small vocal ensembles during the strike. Sinatra came to represent a new phenomenon, the teen idol. The stylings of Sinatra and other pop vocalists caught on at the expense of swing and its instrumental arrangements.

A new form of jazz was also developing during World War II. Small combos began playing music with a harder edge that came to be known as bebop. It would never prove as popular as

swing with the general public, but it defined jazz during the latter half of the 1940s. It also became the basis for modern jazz.

The swing bands never again enjoyed the same level of popularity as they did before the war. Many of the lesser ones disbanded and their members went on to other careers. Artists like Benny Goodman and Artie Shaw survived but experienced lean years. Goodman's career, though, was helped greatly by a successful 1955 Hollywood movie, *The Benny Goodman Story.*

There has always been a strong note of sentimentality in swing music. In particular, the lyrics performed by swing-band singers were often drenched in it. This sentimentality mixed with nostalgia to help make swing music somewhat popular again as its original fans reached middle age. They could tune into television programs like the one featuring Lawrence Welk and his band to tap their feet and fondly remember their younger days.

Even today—decades after most of the famous swing band-leaders have died away—orchestras bearing their names tour the country. In some cases, a son or grandson of the original leader directs the band. These groups and their original recordings help keep swing alive.

The Swing Legacy

Although the swing era came and went in 10 years, it enjoys a continuing legacy. When many older Americans are asked about jazz, they first think of swing music. They are as likely to mention Benny Goodman or Glenn Miller as a top jazz artist as they are Louis Armstrong, Charlie Parker, or Miles Davis.

This makes some jazz purists shake their heads. They see much swing as watered-down and inferior. Some do not even recognize it as real jazz. This is probably overly harsh, but it does tarnish swing's reputation.

Swing has at least one other legacy. Some bandleaders like Benny Goodman also fronted combos (small jazz ensembles). In fact, Goodman's 1938 Carnegie Hall concert featured both his big band and quartet. The roots of modern jazz come more from the quartet heard that night.

Such swing combos set the model for the next era of jazz. As big bands started to die out in the 1940s, small bebop ensembles replaced them, taking the improvisatory essence of the swing combos to new artistic heights.

Duke Ellington and Count Basie

JAZZ NOBILITY

There are many nicknames in jazz. Louis Armstrong was known as Satchmo. Rotund saxophonist Julian Adderley was called Cannonball. Bebop legend Charlie Parker supposedly became known as Yardbird after hitting a chicken with a car.

Occasionally, an artist will earn a nickname that shows something else. It reflects respect paid by fellow musicians. At the highest level, we find a few musicians who have even been elevated to the status of royalty. One of these is the New Orleans musician King Oliver.

Two swing musicians stand as the most famous members of this jazz aristocracy. Duke Ellington is in fact one of the most respected jazz artists of all time. He brought unmatched sophistication and variety to the art of jazz composition. He also led one of the greatest jazz orchestras ever.

In terms of stature, only one band came close to matching

the Ellington orchestra. It was headed by that other nobleman of jazz, Count Basie. While Basie's music may not have matched Ellington's in terms of sophistication, it arguably swung harder.

Birth of a Great Composer

"Music is my mistress and she plays second fiddle to no one." —DUKE ELLINGTON

Edward Kennedy Ellington (1899–1974) was not aristocratic by birth. His family certainly treated him as if he were, though. Ellington's parents so adored him that little Edward did not remember his feet touching the ground until he was six years old.

The Ellingtons lived as a middle class black family in Washington, DC. Edward was nonetheless taught to appreciate the finer things in life. His mother also made sure that he learned correct manners and to act with sophistication and dignity. He would show these traits throughout his life.

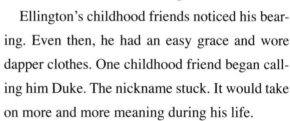

Ellington's childhood friends noticed his bearing. Even then, he had an easy grace and wore dapper clothes. One childhood friend began calling him Duke. The nickname stuck. It would take on more and more meaning during his life.

Ellington's family was musical, and Edward was sent to take piano lessons from the age of seven. Surprisingly, he did not excel at the instrument. He actually remembered skipping more lessons than he attended. Music was just not much of an interest to him as a child. He liked baseball more.

What appealed to Ellington later as a teenager was secretly going to Frank Holiday's pool hall. He apparently learned to play the game quite well. At the hall, Ellington heard pianists performing for patrons. Their ragtime playing was the first music to truly inspire him.

ELLINGTON'S EARLIEST MUSIC

While still in high school, Ellington worked as a soda jerk (a person who serves soft drinks and ice cream at a soda fountain) at a Washington café. He named his first composition after the experience. He composed "Soda Fountain Rag" by ear and learned to play it in a number of popular styles.

In his autobiography, Ellington remembers performing "Soda Fountain Rag" as "a one-step, two-step, waltz, tango, and fox trot. Listeners never knew it was the same piece." They did, however, notice Ellington – especially the girls. He liked the attention. He began to take music more seriously.

At school, Ellington studied music theory. He also learned by watching other pianists. A new style of playing inspired him most. The essence of stride piano playing is found in the left hand. The player hops back and forth between playing bass notes on beats 1 and 3 of each measure and chords on 2 and 4. This leaves the right hand free to play melodies and improvise.

Fresh out of high school, Ellington took a job painting signs. He would ask customers if they had already hired a band when he painted signs for parties and dances. Soon, he was heading up The Duke's Serenaders, a group that played at society balls and even embassy parties in Washington.

Ellington and his ensemble played for both white and black audiences. Such a thing was extremely rare in that segregated age. It helped that he was playing in a cosmopolitan city with an international population. Ellington both played the piano and led the group, as he would throughout his career.

THE DUKE OF HARLEM

In 1922, Ellington left behind a thriving music career in Washington to move to New York City. It was perfect timing. This was just as Fletcher Henderson's band was starting to heat up Harlem. The move also landed Ellington in the middle of the Harlem Renaissance.

This cultural and artistic explosion saw great developments by African-American authors, poets, musicians, intellectuals, and more. In particular, literature blossomed. It was a vibrant time and place that strongly embraced jazz as the music of black America.

By 1924, Ellington was playing regularly in New York and even making records. A year later, he was leading Duke Ellington and his Kentucky Club Orchestra at an establishment of the same name. He quickly become known for compositions, like "Harlem Air Shaft," that captured the vibrancy of the city and even mimicked some of its sounds.

SUGGESTED LISTENING

DUKE ELLINGTON
"Black and Tan Fantasy"
"Diminuendo and Crescendo in Blue"
"It Don't Mean a Thing (If It Ain't Got that Swing)"
"Satin Doll"
"Take the 'A' Train"

COUNT BASIE
"One O'Clock Jump"
"Jumpin' at the Woodside"
"Lester Leaps In"

1927 was a big year for Ellington. He and his group became the house band at the famous Cotton Club. This Harlem hotspot featured black entertainers but catered to an exclusively white audience. The acts too often played to racial stereotypes of the times.

Whatever the downside, weekly broadcasts from the Cotton Club helped make the Duke well known. The radio performances also allowed him to cross America's racial divide, just as Benny Goodman had done, but in the opposite direction.

Around the same time, Ellington entered into a longstanding

relationship with music publisher Irving Mills. The Duke signed over nearly half of his earnings to him, but Mills was a very effective promoter. Their combined talents steadily built Ellington into a prominent figure in the world of jazz.

The Duke and his ensemble provided all of the music for the revues at the Cotton Club. This gave them experience playing a wide variety of styles. The group became especially well known for their hot arrangements and "jungle music" (jazz arrangements that supposedly incorporated African elements).

Birth of a Great Jazz Orchestra

"The most important thing I look for in a musician is whether he knows how to listen." —DUKE ELLINGTON

Ellington's Cotton Club engagement ended in 1931, as the worst of the Great Depression was setting in. The Duke survived much of the decade by taking to the road with his band. He also changed with the times.

Chapter 4 revealed the 1930s to be the swing era. Ellington adapted to the new style of jazz early on and even penned one of its unofficial anthems. The Duke composed "It Don't Mean a Thing (If It Ain't Got that Swing)" in 1931 and first recorded it in 1932. Ellington later wrote that the song proudly shouts out "a sentiment which prevailed among jazz musicians at the time." It still does.

"It Don't Mean a Thing" swings hard from its very first measure. A walking string bass repeats a descending line while the rest of the rhythm section punctuates the backbeats. The female singer, Ivie Anderson, coolly scats, "Wat dat doo, wat dat doo, wat dat doo dat dat doo datta doo."

The musical groove is wonderfully syncopated. It also relies on the relaxed subdivision of the beat that will come to define swing. This clearly sets "It Don't Mean a Thing" apart from the traditional jazz that had reigned through the 1920s.

Duke Ellington

Anderson drops out after the intro and passes the baton to trumpeter Cootie Williams, who improvises around the melody, growling through a mute. This gives the song some of the hot jungle sound that Ellington's band became known for in the 1920s. Saxophones softly hold out notes that create chords. The brass instruments add stabbing exclamations.

When Anderson comes back in, she proudly shouts the title lyrics. This is a call. Muted brass instruments answer with a phrase that sounds like her scat from the intro. They repeat, "Doo wat, doo wat, doo wat…" in tight syncopation. It seems to say, "Yes, it don't mean a thing if ain't got that swing."

Like many popular songs of the time, the melody of "It Don't Mean a Thing" features a 32-bar AABA structure, in which each section is eight measures long. The main part is in the A sections, while B serves as a bridge between them. But there is also something of the blues in "It Don't Mean a Thing." You hear it in the melody—in particular, the blue notes (minor intervals set against major chords) Anderson sings on the word "ain't."

After Anderson sings through the AABA form, alto saxophonist Johnny Hodges begins an extended solo. Musicians like Hodges and Williams would help define the sound of Ellington's orchestra while establishing themselves among the first full-fledged improvisers in jazz after Louis Armstrong.

DUKE THE COMPOSER

Ellington would begin to build a reputation as a remarkable jazz composer during the 1930s. Part of his secret was writing for the musical personalities of band members like Hodges and Williams. In fact, it is often difficult to imagine any musicians playing Ellington's arrangements other than the ones in his band.

This was only part of his success, though. Ellington's brilliance as a composer also came from his musical sophistication. You can hear it in "It Don't Mean a Thing." At intervals during Hodges' solo, the band plays tight chromatic chords that make this more than a mere pop ditty.

The end of the recording likewise reveals Ellington's remarkable flair as a composer and arranger. We hear a fun repetition of the "doo wat, doo wat" muted brass phrase hanging over the end of the song. But even that is a false ending. It fades into a chord held by the saxophones and a final plink from the Duke on piano.

The sophistication heard in the "It Don't Mean a Thing" arrangement grew as a prominent trait in Ellington's music over the years. It would even take his music beyond jazz. In fact, the Duke did not refer to his music as jazz but rather American music. This reflected one of his core beliefs. He was known for complimenting people by saying they were "beyond category." His music was the same.

Ellington showed a serious intent as a composer from early in his career. In 1935, the same year that he penned "It Don't Mean a Thing," he also wrote "Creole Rhapsody." This extended composition required both sides of a 78-rpm record when it was first released. It includes changes in key and interludes for the Duke on piano.

"Reminiscing in Tempo," also from 1935, is even more expansive. Ellington wrote its four sections in memory of his mother. This richly orchestrated work expresses both his sorrow at her passing and the joy that she brought him in life.

The Duke was extremely close to his mother, and she remained in his thoughts through his life. At a 70th birthday celebration for him at the White House, Ellington said, "There is no place I would rather be tonight except in my mother's arms."

The 1930s also brought three of the works that would be most closely associated with Ellington. They would all become jazz standards. The earliest was "Mood Indigo" (1930). Its beautiful combination of high muted trombones and low bass clarinet heard in the melody was striking for that era.

The equally tranquil "In a Sentimental Mood" comes from 1935. It features an interesting harmonic technique known as *line cliché* (a chromatic descending line). The song quickly became a hit of the swing era.

Other well-known works written, co-written, or recorded by Ellington during this period include "Perdido," "Caravan," "Solitude," and "I Got It Bad (And That Ain't Good)." Such standards make up an important part of Ellington's musical legacy.

ENTER BILLY STRAYHORN

In 1939, Ellington started a close collaboration with a younger composer, Billy Strayhorn (1915–1967). Their working relationship would last for decades. Ellington called Sweet Pea, as Strayhorn was known, "my right arm, my left arm, all the eyes in the back of my head."

Strayhorn served Ellington in a number of capacities. He arranged many of the Duke's works and even filled in for Ellington on piano and in front of the band. He co-wrote a number of songs and was a composer in his own right. His biggest hit came in 1941 with "Take the 'A' Train." It has since become one of the best known of all jazz standards.

Strayhorn used his classical training to help Ellington continue his pursuit of jazz as "serious" music. The result can be heard in "Black, Brown, and Beige." It is an ambitious three-movement jazz

LIVES AND TIMES

Harlem Renaissance With the prosperity that followed World War I, the section of Manhattan known as Harlem saw a flowering of black culture. Famous artists of various types—including jazz musicians like Duke Ellington and Fats Waller—made important contributions. The renaissance would continue into the 1930s.

State Department Tours After World War II, the State Department began organizing overseas tours by American musical acts. A primary goal was to promote friendship with America through sharing one of our greatest assets, jazz. The program continues to this day and now includes other forms of American music.

Segregation Jim Crow laws institutionalized racial segregation throughout much of the United States into the 1960s. While jazz artists like Duke Ellington and Count Basie experienced inequality, their music crossed color lines. This played a roll in helping bring down the walls of segregation over time.

symphony that was debuted at Ellington's first Carnegie Hall performance, in 1943.

ELLINGTON IN THE 1940s AND '50s

Ellington's 1940s band was perhaps his finest. It featured a line-up of luminaries that included saxophonists Ben Webster and Johnny Hodges, trumpeter Ray Nance, and, briefly, contrabassist Jimmy Blanton. Despite the talent, the Duke's popularity suffered as bebop caught on at the expense of swing.

Ellington endured tough times into the mid-1950s. Musical salvation came with a legendary performance at the Newport Jazz Festival in 1956. The highlight was the band's playing of "Diminuendo and Crescendo in Blue."

The performance featured a six-minute solo by saxophonist Paul Gonsalves and ended with ear-piercing trumpet high notes from Cat Anderson. The performance caused outright pandemonium among festivalgoers and helped land Ellington on the cover of *Time* magazine a month later.

This success set the stage for Ellington's new role as a senior statesman of jazz. He recorded with a number of other artists, including Ella Fitzgerald and John Coltrane. The Duke also capitalized on European ardor for jazz by touring the continent. Meanwhile, he and Strayhorn scored the music for two Hollywood movies, *Anatomy of a Murder* (1959) and *Paris Blues* (1961).

THE DUKE'S LATE PERIOD

Ellington remained musically vital through the rest of his life. Starting in 1965, he composed and staged three "Sacred Concerts." Ellington referred to these religious works as "the most

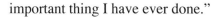

important thing I have ever done."

As befits royalty, Ellington received a number of governmental accolades during this final period. Richard Nixon conferred upon him the Presidential Medal of Freedom in 1969, and the French government awarded him its highest civilian award, the Legion of Honor, in 1973.

The Duke passed away the next year. Headlines around the world marked the death of this noble jazz figure. During her eulogy of Ellington at his funeral, Ella Fitzgerald observed, "A genius has passed." He was indeed a genius, one beyond category.

Basie Jumps In

"If you play a tune and a person don't tap their feet, don't play the tune." —COUNT BASIE

Duke Ellington brought unparalleled sophistication to jazz, but it was another member of the jazz aristocracy who taught it how to really swing. Pianist William "Count" Basie (1904–1984) led one of the hottest jazz orchestras anywhere for nearly half a century.

With the help of extraordinary musicians like saxophonist Lester Young and trumpeter Harry "Sweets" Edison, as well as singers Jimmy Rushing and Joe Williams, the Basie band swung furiously. It established a legacy for the Count as one of the greatest jazz bandleaders of all time.

Basie grew up in Red Bank, New Jersey, about 50 miles outside of New York City. His upbringing was more ordinary than Duke Ellington's, but the two shared a teenage desire for the grownup world. Whereas the Duke hung out at Frank Holiday's poolroom, the Count frequented his local vaudeville theatre.

The Duke and the Count shared something else. Both had mothers that made sure they took piano lessons. The training paid off for Basie when he was 15. One day, the theatre's regular pianist failed to show up to accompany a silent movie. Basie filled in and before long was playing for an assortment of local gigs.

By the time he was 20, Basie had moved to New York City, where he got to know and learn from some of the best stride pianists of the day, including Willie "The Lion" Smith and Fats Waller. Soon, he was accompanying shows and playing at Leroy's, a nightspot known for its hot pianists.

BASIE IN KANSAS CITY

Basie found himself stranded in Kansas City while touring with a vaudeville show in 1927. To survive in the Midwest, he began playing with area bands including one led by Bennie Moten. In the Moten band, Basie mastered a forceful style of early swing playing known as stomp. He also met Ben Webster, the great tenor saxophonist mentioned earlier.

After Moten's death, in 1935, Basie began leading a small ensemble of former mates from Moten's band. The group included two musicians who would become legendary jazz figures, drummer Jo Jones and tenor saxophonist Lester Young.

Live radio broadcasts from Kansas City of Basie's new band were important in two ways: First, Basie became immortalized as the Count when a broadcaster used the nickname to introduce him on air one night. Also, influential music industry figure John Hammond heard one of the broadcasts.

Hammond inspired Basie and his band to move to New York in 1936. He also helped them quickly build a national following.

The timing could not have been more perfect; Benny Goodman had just created a national craze for swing music.

ONE O'CLOCK JUMP

The Count's first hit tune, "One O'Clock Jump," is also the one most closely associated with him. It reveals a style that is very different from that of Duke Ellington. In the Duke's recordings,

Count Basie

we find a meticulous writer of finely crafted compositions. With "One O'Clock Jump," we have a song that simply evolved out of the band's improvised riffs (short repeated phrases) at a gig one night.

Other prominent Basie traits are heard in the original 1937 recording of "One O'Clock Jump." The number begins with Basie on piano playing a bluesy, swinging riff that leads into two choruses of an improvised stride solo.

Jazz musicians often say that a band is "cooking" when the music is really swinging. Basie's rhythm section cooks hard throughout the recording. Many Basie numbers follow this model. The leader begins the piece with a piano solo; the rhythm section enters and swings away mightily.

The jump style and riff-based nature of "One O'Clock Jump" are also classic Basie. Most of the piece is just a swinging blues jam with a collection of riffs, which underscore improvised solos by different band members.

The centerpiece of the recording is a wonderful solo duel between the band's two tenor saxophone players, Herschel Evans and Lester Young. Young's smoking, nuanced repetition of the same notes at the beginning of his solo is classic.

The main melody of "One O'Clock Jump" does not enter until after all of the solos are finished. It is nearly two minutes and 30 seconds into the recording. Even then, the melody is riff-like. It makes the performance sound spontaneous and more like the product of collective creativity than composition.

The Count enjoyed success throughout the rest of the 1930s and into the 1940s. Like Benny Goodman and his group, he took part in a celebrated battle of the bands against Chick Webb and his ensemble at the Savoy Ballroom. Basie lost. No matter, his career soared and he was hugely influential; Goodman even played "One O'Clock Jump" as part of his famous 1938 Carnegie Hall concert.

The rest of Basie's career paralleled that of Duke Ellington in a number of ways. He first weathered a career downturn in the early 1950s as the popularity of swing died out. The Count

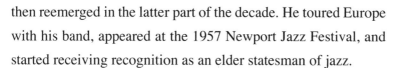

then reemerged in the latter part of the decade. He toured Europe with his band, appeared at the 1957 Newport Jazz Festival, and started receiving recognition as an elder statesman of jazz.

Although highly respected, Basie never received the full adulation reserved for Ellington and other jazz immortals. He and his band just kept jumping and swinging until almost the very end of his life, in 1984.

The Legacy of Ellington and Basie

The Duke and the Count share a jazz legacy to a certain extent. Both headed up swing bands of African-American musicians that proved popular across the country's racial divide. This was important. Jazz has always come most potently from the black community. Indeed, most of its highly influential artists have been black.

With the coming of swing and white artists like Benny Goodman, Glenn Miller, and Artie Shaw, jazz also became the music of white America. This spread its popularity across the entire country. However, it also threatened its authenticity. But artists like Ellington and Basie helped keep swing rooted in the experience of black America.

Beyond this, the musical legacies of the Duke and the Count are quite different. Ellington represents perhaps the finest composer in the jazz tradition. He took the music far beyond what it might have otherwise been. In fact, the Duke preferred to call his works simply American music rather than jazz. On the other hand, Basie represents the very essence of swing music. He had no problem with his music being called jazz, and jazz meant one thing for him: swing.

Charlie Parker

BIRD AND BEBOP

Jazz artists enjoy playing with language almost as much as with sound. In fact, quite a bit of modern American slang comes from jazz. *Bread* means money, *cool* means great or sublime, and *crib* means a place where you dwell. You can also refer to a person as man. Put them all together and you get, "Man, what a cool crib. Did it cost a lot of bread?"

Jazz has also brought us novel terms to describe new ways of making music. The term scat was coined for vocal improvisation using nonsense syllables. In turn, scat singing may have given us the name for a new form of jazz that emerged during the 1940s: bebop.

Scat vocalists of the 1930s used distinctive syllables to capture the mood of swing music. *Wat dat doo* seems to perfectly capture the musical feel of "It Don't Mean a Thing." In the 1940s, a younger group of musicians began experimenting with a style of jazz with a harder edge, featuring music with big melodic leaps that scatted words like *bebop* or *rebop* seemed to fit.

Bebop (or simply bop) developed into the dominant type of jazz during the latter half of the 1940s. It replaced the big bands and dance rhythms of swing with small combos playing music often much too fast for dance. Bebop was less music for light entertainment or dancing and more for serious listening. It also brought us the next true genius of jazz: Charlie Parker.

The Origins of Bebop

He didn't worry about anything else as long as he could play that horn. —JAY MCSHANN ON CHARLIE PARKER

Sometimes history seems to hinge on a single event. A remarkable person stands in the right place at the right time. A chance meeting takes place. An assassin strikes down an important figure. Single events have had a major impact on the history of jazz as well. One clearly made way for bebop's development.

In 1942, the American Federation of Musicians struck against the nation's major record labels over royalties. The timing was terrible. The country had just entered World War II. American sympathy was hardly with union musicians over more pay.

There was another problem for the AFM. It only represented instrumentalists, not vocalists. So, swing bands did not record during the two years of the strike, but vocalists continued to do so. This allowed singers like Frank Sinatra to emerge as stars.

Vocal records took the place of instrumentals by Benny Goodman and Glenn Miller on store shelves and radio stations across the country. America's taste in music changed as a result. Swing

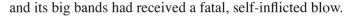

and its big bands had received a fatal, self-inflicted blow.

While this was the major cause of swing's decline, other factors also played a part. For one, the war led to domestic rationing of gasoline and rubber for tires. This made it difficult for big bands to tour the country for live performances.

Many young jazz musicians were not available anyway since they had joined the military. A young soldier stationed overseas in England could hear Glenn Miller perform more easily than his sweetheart at home.

Waiting in the wings during all of this were younger jazz musicians. The commercialism of swing did not interest them. Instead, they found inspiration among more adventurous jazz figures active in the 1930s. They especially liked the playing of pianists Art Tatum and Earl "Fatha" Hines.

Tenor saxophonists Lester Young and Coleman Hawkins also served as guiding lights for the younger players. In particular, they prized Hawkins' 1939 recording of "Body and Soul," featuring an improvisation with pitch choices that were quite daring for the time. At times, Hawkins even seemed to play at double the tempo of his backing ensemble.

AN UNDERGROUND SOUND

A young saxophonist would take these innovations and fashion them into something wholly new. Like Hawkins, Charlie Parker (1920–1955) was from the Midwest. Unlike him, he preferred the alto to the tenor saxophone. Parker took up the instrument in school and started playing jazz and blues publicly in Kansas City during the days of Benny Moten and Count Basie. (See Chapter 5.)

Legends exist about how much time the young Parker spent

learning to play. Some say he practiced up to 16 hours a day and would play songs by ear in every possible key. He obviously took music very seriously.

By 1940, Parker had left Kansas City for New York. It took him a while to catch on in the big city. He even washed dishes at a club where piano giant Art Tatum played. Soon enough, though, Parker wound up in an orchestra led by pianist Jay McShann.

It was during this time that Parker seems to have gotten his nickname, Yardbird, often shortened to Bird. McShann remembered Parker yelling out when they hit a chicken with their car on tour, "Back up. You hit a yardbird!" Apparently, Parker enjoyed chicken so much that he had the bird cooked and then ate it whole that night.

Parker next found himself in the orchestra of Earl Hines, who had played with Louis Armstrong in Chicago. In the band, Charlie got to know trumpeter Dizzy Gillespie. The two would go on to become frequent collaborators and among the main architects of bebop.

Unfortunately, Bird displayed an irresponsible streak throughout his career. With the Hines band, he simply could not make it to performances on time. He wound up getting fired.

Parker's addiction to drugs and alcohol no doubt had a lot to do with his delinquency. It was an unbreakable habit that started while he was on morphine in a hospital after a car accident. It continued for the rest of his life.

A lot of live jazz by small groups continued in New York during the 1942–1944 AFM strike. Much of it was underground and experimental. It

SUGGESTED LISTENING

CHARLIE PARKER
"April in Paris"
"Anthropology"
"Donna Lee"
"Groovin' High"
"Ko-Ko"
"Scrapple from the Apple"
"Yardbird Suite"

DIZZY GILLESPIE
"A Night in Tunisia"
"Salt Peanuts"

THELONIOUS MONK
"'Round Midnight"
"Monk's Mood"
"Straight, No Chaser"

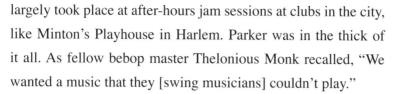

largely took place at after-hours jam sessions at clubs in the city, like Minton's Playhouse in Harlem. Parker was in the thick of it all. As fellow bebop master Thelonious Monk recalled, "We wanted a music that they [swing musicians] couldn't play."

By 1945, the underground experimenters were making their way above ground. Charlie was leading his own jazz combo with Dizzy Gillespie. They performed at the trendiest jazz clubs in New York. Many of these were on 52nd Street, and it became the epicenter for the bebop that was now clearly emerging.

The Birth of Modern Jazz

They teach you there's a boundary line to music. But, man, there's no boundary line to art.—CHARLIE PARKER

So what was this new style of jazz? What was bebop? Parker supposedly hit upon a main element during a jam session one night in 1939. He apparently had been trying to find this ingredient for some time. He later remembered, "I kept thinking there's bound to be something else. I could hear it sometimes, but I couldn't play it."

What Bird happened upon was a way of improvising that is difficult to explain. Jazz improvisation takes place over chords played by a rhythm section. Before bebop, the chords used were fairly simple and straightforward. Each one had just three or four notes. However, chords can be extended and/or altered to have seven or more notes, creating more complex-sounding structures.

Parker discovered that he could play what he had been hearing by incorporating such extended chord tones into his improvisations. As he put it, "I realized by using the high notes of the chords as a melodic line, and by the right harmonic progression, I could play what I heard inside me. That's when I was born."

This musical feat, small as it might seem, was downright revolutionary. It made the music sound quite different, much less tuneful and much more tart and angular. The chordal complexities resulted in improvisations that were almost the sonic equivalent of Picasso paintings, marking the beginning of what we call modern jazz.

Like most revolutions, bebop drew mixed reactions from jazz musicians and fans. Some welcomed the harmonic development at the heart of bebop. Others rejected it. Duke Ellington even said, "Playing bop is like playing Scrabble with all the vowels missing."

Bebop artists did not seem to care about such criticism. They just referred to unsupportive predecessors as moldy figs.

Jazz had reached a crucial turning point. Bebop was all about the music and the artists who made it. Swing was much more for the enjoyment of listeners and dancers. Bebop had little use for such "squares." Art stood as the important thing for hardcore bebop musicians.

FAST AND FURIOUS

Bebop brought with it other changes. For one, it favored faster tempos than those found in swing. Some compositions, like Parker's "Ko-Ko," even race along at a frantic, furious pace. This did not present a problem since bebop was music more for listening than dancing.

The melodies of many original bebop works were also different. They were less tuneful than swing melodies. In large part, this came from the same emphasis on chord extensions found in bebop improvisation.

Many bebop melodies flitter and twist like a butterfly in flight. Others, like "Salt Peanuts," are filled with large, jagged intervals, which give the music a particularly modern sound.

While such melodies may have been contemporary, many of the chord progressions they pranced above were old school. In fact, dozens of bebop pieces incorporated stock progressions from just a few popular songs, like the 1930 George Gershwin hit "I Got Rhythm," known as rhythm changes.

Bebopers would frequently tinker with these stock progressions, though. Chord substitutions using harmonic extensions and alterations became common. Often, pianists would make these substitutions spontaneously during a performance. This became central to the sound of modern jazz.

LIVES AND TIMES

AFM Strike In 1942, the union representing instrumental musicians struck against record companies over royalties. The industry responded by releasing albums featuring popular vocalists like Frank Sinatra. The union effort backfired and helped bring an end to the swing era.

Baby Boom The prosperity that followed World War II brought an increase in the birth rate that lasted for almost two decades. Known as baby boomers, those born during this period helped shape many developments in American culture.

Beat Generation The beat poets of the 1950s prized passionate, unrestrained expression. Members included Allen Ginsberg, William S. Burroughs and Jack Kerouac. They took much inspiration from bebop and the lives of its artists.

NEW COMBO CONFIGURATIONS

The role of the jazz rhythm section changed with bebop. Drummers started to propel groups forward with patterns of swinging eighth notes on the ride cymbal. Bass players continued to lay down walking lines but with more complexities than in earlier forms of jazz. Pianists, for their part, abandoned stride in favor of playing block chords in syncopated rhythm known as comping.

Bebop also featured small ensembles, not big bands like in swing. A typical bop combo featured the sort of rhythm section just described, sometimes with the addition of a guitar. In front, you would usually find only one or two wind instruments, most often, trumpet and/or saxophone.

Most important, Bebop became a vehicle for improvisation. Written arrangements were central to swing, with improvisation usually playing a limited role. Bebop turned this relationship inside out. The set melody for a piece became little more than a pretext for improvisation.

BILLIE'S BOUNCE

You can hear all of these musical facets in one of the first bebop recordings. Charlie Parker recorded his original piece "Billie's Bounce" in 1945 with a legendary group of artists that included Miles Davis on trumpet, Max Roach on drums, Dizzy Gillespie on piano rather than trumpet, and Curley Russell on bass.

Following a very brief piano intro, Parker and Davis enter playing the melody of "Billie's Bounce" in harmony. Behind them, Roach lays down a swinging pattern on the ride cymbal, and Gillespie plays short, stabbing chords on piano. As the melody unfolds, it becomes clear the piece rests atop a 12-bar progression of blues chords.

Parker and Davis play the head of "Billie's Bounce" twice. Then, Parker launches into an improvised solo that lasts for four repetitions of the 12-bar structure. All the while, Roach's ride cymbal rings out, Gillespie comps away on piano, and Russell keeps on walking.

Jazz artists to this day revere Parker's improvisations. They study them intensely and memorize many of the licks that Parker

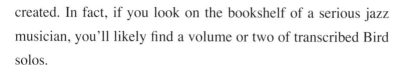

created. In fact, if you look on the bookshelf of a serious jazz musician, you'll likely find a volume or two of transcribed Bird solos.

Parker's improvisation on "Billie's Bounce" is considered to be among his greatest efforts. He does a masterful job of being bluesy while forging new musical ground. In particular, the double-time lick at the end of his second chorus is true Bird.

One might say that the chord extensions that Parker plays at the beginning of his fourth improvised chorus are "out there." It almost sounds as if he's playing in the wrong key. This does not last for long. Bird masterfully steps back into the key and finishes off his solo with several of his trademark riffs, filled with charm and a bluesy air.

Davis immediately follows Bird with two improvised choruses on trumpet. About five measures in, he lands on a chord extension with a noticeable sting to it. In the background, you can hear Dizzy comp a chord with equal bite. It is a wonderful moment.

Davis would grow to become one of the most influential musicians in the history of jazz. At this 1945 session, though, he is still very young. His solo is interesting, but he is obviously a young rookie next to Parker.

YARDBIRD'S DEMISE

Sadly, the mid-1940s marked a high point for the Yardbird. During his remaining years, Parker fought addiction to continue making music. He often lost the struggle and would even sell his horn more than once to feed his habit. The year after recording "Billie's Bounce," he found himself committed for six months to Camarillo State Mental Hospital, in California. (Parker pays tribute to the institution in his tune "Relaxin' at Camarillo.")

By the 1950s, though, Parker had earned recognition as a leading jazz figure. Other musicians were starting to imitate his style and steal his licks. It must have been cold comfort for Bird, who continued to record and perform while burdened by his problems.

Parker died long before his time, in 1955, at the age of 34. The hard life that led to his early end now made him a symbol. He had become a Van Gogh of jazz, a tormented genius who died for his art. Famed director and jazz fan Clint Eastwood even immortalized Bird in a Hollywood biopic. Parker may be gone but his music endures. Bird lives!

Boppin' Along

I hit the piano with my elbow sometimes because of a certain sound I want to hear, certain chords. —THELONIOUS MONK

No other name is more closely associated with bebop than Charlie Parker's. However, other talented artists helped develop the style. We've already looked at Dizzy Gillespie. He had a different and much longer career than Bird. We'll return to him in our chapter on Latin jazz. We will also come back to Miles Davis.

Pianist Thelonious Monk (1917–1982) is another towering figure in the history of bebop. A true original, both Monk and his music had an unmistakable style all their own. Monk stabbed at the piano keys using technique that would make a classically trained pianist cringe. He sat askew on the bench, his foot stomping the floor. His solos featured clusters of notes and often seemed more like compositions in themselves than impromptu

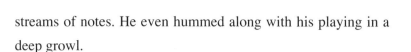

streams of notes. He even hummed along with his playing in a deep growl.

Monk was born and raised in North Carolina. By 1941, he was jamming away at Minton's Playhouse in Harlem with such greats as guitarist and Benny Goodman alumnus Charlie Christian and trumpeter Roy Eldridge. Monk would go on to become the house pianist at this important incubator of bebop.

Fellow pianist Mary Lou Williams remembered an even younger Monk she rubbed shoulders with in Kansas City. "He had ideas even then that were way ahead of his time. He was one of the original modernists all right, playing pretty much the

Charlie Rouse with Thelonious Monk

same harmonies then that he's playing now," she recalled in the 1950s.

Williams called these musical experiments by Monk and others "zombie music"— "Because the screwy chords reminded us of music from *Frankenstein* or any horror film," she said.

Monk was equally original when it came to his dress. He set the style for bebop musicians wearing berets. He even designed a pair of heavy-framed glasses that became his trademark. According to Williams, Monk was the sharpest of the sharp when it came to dress. Fans who imitated Monk's style and other bebop fashion came to be known as hipsters.

Blue Note is one of the most important jazz record companies. Founded in 1939, the label—along with others, like Prestige and Verve—became central to the development of bebop. Artists such as Miles Davis, Milt Jackson, Clifford Brown, and James Moody all recorded for Blue Note.

Monk's first recording for Blue Note came in 1947. It included a young Art Blakey on drums. Through 1954, Monk made a number of landmark recordings for Blue Note with various top musicians, eventually released in an anthology called *Genius of Modern Music*. The title said it all.

STRAIGHT, NO CHASER

Volume 2 of *Genius of Modern Music* contains one of Monk's best-known compositions, "Straight, No Chaser." The original recording of the piece begins with Art Blakey on drums laying down a sizzling, swinging pattern on ride cymbal. He punctuates it with a series of syncopated rim shots on the snare drum.

Monk then enters on piano with the melody, syncopated and angular, constructed from a single riff. Somehow, it seems to distill the entire essence of bebop into just five notes. Played over a 12-bar blues progression, it is pure Monk.

On the second chorus, saxophone and vibraphone take over the melody. On the vibes is Milt Jackson, another musician closely associated with Blue Note at the time. Jackson would become best known as part of the influential Modern Jazz Quartet.

There is a contrast in styles among the improvised solos that follow. Monk goes first; his approach feels original and progressive, a perfect match for the feel of the piece. The same is true for Jackson's solo. Sahib Shihab's saxophone improvisation, though, sounds imitative, like he is trying too hard to channel the spirit of Charlie Parker.

Milt Jackson

"Straight, No Chaser" ends with a single return to the melody. The whole thing clocks in at just three minutes, but says so much in that brief span of time. "Straight, No Chaser" quickly became a jazz standard. It has been rerecorded by such jazz giants as Miles Davis and Cannonball Adderley and remains a favorite among jazz musicians to this day.

HARD BOP

Thelonious Monk continued to perform and record extensively through the 1960s. Starting in the 1970s, he withdrew almost entirely from public life. Mental illness was the likely cause. During his final years, he wound up in New Jersey as a guest of the British-born Baroness Pannonica "Nica" de Koenigswarter,

a patron of jazz who also sheltered Charlie Parker in his last days.

In the mid-1950s, Monk became associated with hard bop. This offshoot of bebop countered another style, cool jazz, which had developed a few years earlier. Hard bop mixed bebop with influences from outside of the jazz mainstream, like rhythm and blues and gospel.

Monk soon moved past hard bop to continue blazing his own idiosyncratic path in music. Other pioneers remained with the style. Pianist Horace Silver and drummer Art Blakey are two of the artists most closely associated with hard bop. Together, they headed a series of groups during the first half of the 1950s. Calling themselves the Jazz Messengers, they helped develop hard bop as a style. Silver went on to record a number of hard bop classics on his own, including "Sister Sadie" and "The Preacher."

Blakey continued leading the Jazz Messengers for the rest of a long career. Not only did it stand as a continuing testament to hard bop, it served as a launching pad for many young jazz musicians. In fact, alumni from the Jazz Messengers make up something of a who's who of jazz during the past several decades. The list includes pianists Keith Jarrett and Cedar Walton, trumpeters Donald Byrd and Wynton Marsalis, and saxophonists Wayne Shorter and Marsalis' brother Branford.

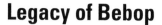

Legacy of Bebop

By the mid-1950s, bebop was already on its way out as the dominant force in jazz. Fresh styles of jazz like hard bop and cool jazz, which you'll read more about shortly, had come along. A new music, rock 'n' roll, also captivated America. The complexities and hard-edged sound of bebop kept it from ever gaining a mass audience like swing. Rock 'n' roll was much more elemental. Like swing, it was also dance music. With the birth of rock, jazz ceased being the main popular music of the country.

Bebop continued to have a large influence for a few more years among members of the so-called Beat Generation—a group of American writers like Allen Ginsberg and Jack Kerouac who opposed the norms of American society.

It was more than bebop music that enthused these artists and their followers, known as beatniks. They also idealized its musicians and their lifestyle; they peppered their language with bebop slang. Some even wore berets and dark sun glasses in imitation of Monk and others.

In a broad sense, the influence of bebop has never died among jazz musicians. Many of the pieces first performed by the likes of Parker, Gillespie, and Monk remain standards. Bebop continues as part of the fabric of today's jazz in other ways. You can hear it in chord progressions and the Charlie Parker licks that musicians still work into their improvisations. In important ways, bebop now represents the common practice of jazz—the language on which modern idioms are built and the first vocabulary that many budding jazz musicians learn.

Ella Fitzgerald

THE JAZZ SINGERS

When we think of jazz, we naturally think of all the great in-strumentalists. We imagine the likes of Louis Armstrong, Benny Goodman, Charlie Parker, Miles Davis, John Coltrane, and Art Tatum. This is for good reason. Every single style of jazz has been instrumental at heart.

At the same time, singers have also made important contribu-tions to jazz throughout its history. We have already looked at the recordings Louis Armstrong made as a vocalist, and Chapter 5 discussed the singers who performed with big bands during the swing era. As we shall see here, singers have played a role in just about every other jazz movement down through the years as well.

It can actually be a little difficult to say what is a jazz singer. This is a topic we have touched upon before. Improvisation is a central part of jazz. With instrumentalists, a person who does not improvise would not normally be considered a jazz musician. Some singers associated with jazz have improvised extensively. Ella Fitzgerald immediately comes to mind, and it is easy to identify her as a jazz artist.

With singers who do not improvise but sing in a jazz style, things become hazier. Billie Holiday is a prime example. She seldom improvised in an out-and-out fashion like a jazz instrumentalist or an Ella Fitzgerald. Yet, she sang in a jazz style and with some of the greatest jazz artists in history.

The First Jazz Vocalists

I'm gonna sing it jazzy.
—AL JOLSON IN *THE JAZZ SINGER*

The 1927 motion picture *The Jazz Singer* proved a smash hit at the box office. This was largely because it featured something new for the time—sound. Up to that point, all but a very few movies had been silent. Live musicians would add appropriate background music in the theaters where movies would play. Otherwise, the only sound made by movies came from the whirring and clacking of the projectors. All of that changed in 1927.

The Jazz Singer starred famed actor Al Jolson (1886–1950). Known as "The World's Greatest Entertainer," Jolson was a consummate showman. He had already become a star through appearances on Broadway and singing on record. His 1920 recording of the George Gershwin song "Swanee" had been a particularly big hit. He had also toured the country to much acclaim with the musical "Bombo."

Jolson's star power helped assure that *The Jazz Singer* was a great success. His life also helped inspire the movie's plotline.

A Jewish-American stage performer is torn between family expectations for him and a desire to sing jazz on stage as a career. So, casting Jolson in the lead for the motion picture made perfect sense.

The Jazz Singer took full advantage of Jolson's musical talents and the new element of sound by incorporating a number of songs. (Actually, there is more singing than spoken dialogue in the movie.) The songs Jolson sings include "My Mammy" and "Toots, Toots, Tootsie (Goodbye)" and Irving Berlin's "Blue Skies."

The onscreen performance of "Blue Skies" is particularly interesting. The character Jolson plays, Jack Robin, performs the song for his mother, accompanying himself on the piano in her parlor. He does so in the ragtime-influenced Broadway style of the time.

After the song, Jack tells his mother all the things he would like to do for her if he's successful as a performer. He then says, "Mama, listen, I'm gonna sing this like I will if I go on the stage, you know, with the show. I'm gonna sing it jazzy. Now get this."

Jolson does indeed jazz up the second performance of "Blue Skies." It still shows the influence of ragtime. However, the song is now faster and more boisterous. Jolson even slaps at the piano keys at one point. He also sings the melody in a more syncopated fashion and improvises around it a bit.

Jack puts on a wonderful demonstration until his father enters and yells, "Stop!" He cannot abide such "uncivilized" music making in his house.

With "Blue Skies," Jolson displays an early style of jazz singing, which had developed since the Original Dixieland Jazz Band started a national craze for jazz in 1917 (see Chapter 2). Soon, jazz bands were crisscrossing the country in the traveling variety shows known as vaudeville.

Jazz bands in vaudeville accompanied singers like Jolson, who had built his career in that theater tradition. Other vaudeville stars, such as Eddie Cantor and Jimmy Durante, also found inspiration in early jazz.

There were actually two worlds of vaudeville at the time, one white and the other black. In the latter, female blues singers like Mamie Smith, Ma Rainey, and Bessie Smith reigned supreme. They may not have been jazz artists, but then again there has always been a close affinity between blues and jazz.

ST. LOUIS BLUES

Blues artists of the 1920s often performed and recorded with jazz musicians. Bessie Smith's 1925 recording of "St. Louis Blues" is

a standout in this regard. The song was written by famous blues composer W.C. Handy and had enjoyed much success since its publication as sheet music about a decade before.

Other artists had recorded "St. Louis Blues" before Smith. It would also go on to become one of the most popular standards for blues and jazz singers alike. Nonetheless, many feel Smith's recording is the definitive version of the song.

Smith's rendition of "St. Louis Blues" achieves a wonderful marriage of blues and jazz. Her singing is definitely that of a blues vocalist. However, jazz icon Louis Armstrong accompanies her on muted cornet, and he definitely brings the jazz to this musical party.

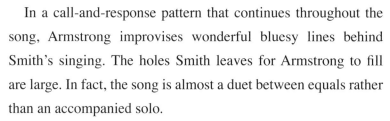

In a call-and-response pattern that continues throughout the song, Armstrong improvises wonderful bluesy lines behind Smith's singing. The holes Smith leaves for Armstrong to fill are large. In fact, the song is almost a duet between equals rather than an accompanied solo.

Blues recordings with jazz artists from the 1920s opened the door for younger jazz singers like Billie Holiday (discussed below), who would come along in the following decade and incorporate blues into their repertoire. The kindred nature of blues and jazz helped make this transition possible.

SATCHMO'S SINGING

It is hard to overestimate the influence of Louis Armstrong in the history of jazz. While we just found him playing cornet behind Bessie Smith, Chapter 3 revealed his influence on traditional jazz and the development of swing. Many also believe Satchmo did more than any other individual to establish the voice as a vehicle for jazz expression.

Armstrong's 1926 recording of "Heebie Jeebies" stands as a milestone. Many cite it as the first recorded example of scat singing. Actually, a few other jazz artists beat Armstrong to that distinction. Al Jolson, for instance, scatted a little in his 1911 recording of "That Haunting Melody."

New Orleans jazz legend Jelly Roll Morton claimed that Armstrong and other early jazz singers actually picked up scat directly or indirectly from a single individual. In an interview, Morton said, "The first man that ever did a scat number in the history of this country was a man from Vicksburg, Mississippi, by the name of Joe Sims, an old comedian."

Whether or not Armstrong invented scat or was even the first to record it, he developed it to a much higher degree than anyone before him. On "Heebie Jeebies," he plays cornet at the beginning of the piece. After a couple of improvised instrumental solos, Armstrong sings the melody for the song with lyrics. He then scats a chorus, improvising with nonsense syllables.

Legend claims that this scat solo was actually accidental. Supposedly, Armstrong dropped the lyric sheet for "Heebie Jeebies" during the recording session and had to freestyle it. Satchmo never confirmed this story, and it probably is not true. However, it is in keeping with the spontaneous character of the solo.

Armstrong's scatting on "Heebie Jeebies" seems to capture the essence of his cornet playing. You can hear it in his phrasing and in the syllables he uses. This instrument-like approach would become a hallmark of Satchmo's scat singing and have a major influence on those who followed in his footsteps. To this day, scat singers often seem to be imitating the sound and phrasing of jazz instrumentalists.

Swing and Beyond

If I'm going to sing like someone else, then I don't need to sing at all. —BILLIE HOLIDAY

Throughout the rest of his career, Armstrong kept on scatting. We have already looked at his wonderful vocal solos on the 1928's "West End Blues" and 1931's "Lazy River." In the same chapter, we learned this was during a time that Satchmo was helping establish a new jazz style known as swing.

Swing fully flowered during the latter half of the 1930s. When it did, a generation of swinging jazz singers emerged. These vocalists typically performed with the big bands that became popular with the style.

The Boswell Sisters began recording in the early 1930s and scored a major hit with a swinging record of "The Object of My Affection" in 1935. This was just as the style was poised to take over the country. It made them quite influential.

The three Boswells hailed from New Orleans, the cradle of jazz. While they were white, their musical influences boldly crossed lines of color. For example, Connee Boswell's 1925 recording of "Cryin' Blues" shows the influence of blues singers like Mamie Smith.

Even before "The Object of My Affection," the Boswell Sisters had become prominent. In particular, Connee, who sang lead, became an inspiration for other vocalists, including a young singer

SUGGESTED LISTENING

BILLIE HOLIDAY
"God Bless the Child"
"Good Morning, Heartache"
"Lover Man"
"Strange Fruit"

ELLA FITZGERALD
"Flying Home"
"Oh, Lady be Good"
"Summertime"

who had grown up in the New York City area. Ella Fitzgerald (1917–1996) would recall, "My mother brought home one of her records, and I fell in love with it."

ELLA

Ella Fitzgerald first dreamed of being a dancer but changed her mind during a 1934 amateur competition at the Harlem's Apollo Theater (an important live venue in the history of black American music). Intimidated by the talent of other dancers on the show, she came onstage and sang two songs made famous by Connee Boswell. Fitzgerald won the contest and found a new artistic direction.

A year later, Fitzgerald began singing with the hottest swing band in New York. The ensemble led by drummer Chick Webb had already been serving as the house band at Harlem's Savoy

Ballroom for several years. Webb's swinging powers were legendary. The addition of Ella Fitzgerald now lent a powerful voice to the ensemble.

In 1938, Fitzgerald enjoyed her first hit single with a jazzy recording of the children's nursery rhyme "A-Tisket, A-Tasket."

LIVES AND TIMES

Swing Era The big bands of the 1930s and 1940s made swing music popular. Many featured excellent vocalists; some, including Ella Fitzgerald and Billie Holiday, became well-known jazz singers.

The Jazz Singer The first "talkie" movie brought sound to film in 1927. A musical, it tells the story of a young man from a conservative background who dreams of singing jazz professionally.

Microphone Before the invention of the modern microphone, singers had to shout their lyrics to fill an auditorium. Similarly, recordings could not capture their vocal nuances. All of that changed as the device became common in the 1930s. Vocalists could now murmur songs and still be heard over a band. This developed into a popular way of singing called crooning.

The following year, Webb passed away. Unexpectedly, Fitzgerald found herself the leader of the ensemble. Renamed Ella Fitzgerald and Her Famous Orchestra, the group performed and recorded together for several years.

When the swing era started to die out in the 1940s, Fitzgerald made a stylistic transition. She embraced the new style of bebop, and it launched her into the next phase of her career.

The change started when Fitzgerald joined the band led by Dizzy Gillespie. She began to improvise scat solos in imitation of Gillespie and other instrumentalists in the group. As she put it, "I just tried to do what I heard the horns in the band doing."

OH, LADY BE GOOD

Two recordings from the 1940s established Fitzgerald as an unparalleled scat singer. The first was of the song "Flying Home," recorded in 1945 and released in 1947. While her scatting is already well developed, the performance is more swing than bebop.

Fitzgerald's 1947 recording of the George Gershwin song

"Oh, Lady Be Good" showed the world her supreme mastery as a scat singer. The horn arrangement still sounds like swing, but Fitzgerald's performance and the harmonic underpinning are bebop through and through.

The first thing a listener notices about "Oh, Lady Be Good" is how Fitzgerald smoothly glides above the band while singing the melody. This clearly reflects bebop; it sounds like how an instrumentalist such as Gillespie or Charlie Parker would play the head for a song like "Yardbird Suite." It gives the performance an understated coolness.

The recording's arrangement is also reflective of bebop. It is in AABA form and relies on a head arrangement. In it, the melody for the song is played at the beginning and the end of the performance. Members of the band improvise over the chord structure associated with the melody during the rest of the recording.

Typically, various members of a band will improvise during a head arrangement. In "Oh, Lady Be Good," it's all Ella all of the time—an astounding tour de force. She adapts the art of instrumental bebop soloing with incredible vocal dexterity and artistic assurance. With a lesser artist, this might sound imitative. Fitzgerald, though, brings bebop soloing to new heights.

In a way, the marriage of scat singing and bebop makes perfect sense. After all, the name of the style itself probably came from horn players trying to imitate their instrumental phrases. In fact, near the end of "Oh, Lady Be Good," Fitzgerald sings one of the scat phrases most closely associated with bebop, "Oo, bop, sh'bam."

Throughout the scat improvisation, one can hear how well Fitzgerald learned "to do what I heard the horns in the band doing." Many of the phrases seem to have come straight from the collective arsenal of Gillespie and Parker. Yet, they are not completely derivative. Fitzgerald, with her depth of artistry, makes them her own.

Ella's playfulness also shines in this performance of "Oh, Lady Be Good." For example, she adds a brief quote from "A-Tisket, A-Tasket" in the bridge of her second improvised chorus. Later, she throws in a little of the bugle call "Reveille." There are also low-pitched growly notes that are not only humorous but show off her large vocal and tonal range.

Fitzgerald would continue to enjoy a long career as a celebrated vocalist. She still stands as the most extraordinary scat singer in the history of jazz. Her purity of tone, perfect sense of pitch, remarkable vocal range, and range of expression remain unparalleled. In the 1970s, commercials by the Memorex Company even featured Ella supposedly breaking a glass with the power of her voice.

LADY DAY

Only one other singer has enjoyed the same status as Ella Fitzgerald in the history of jazz. Billie Holiday (1915–1959) was a very different sort of artist. She did not scat, nor did she possess such remarkable vocal gifts as Fitzgerald. In fact, her range and tone, relatively small to begin with, diminished as her career developed. Despite these limitations, Holiday reigned as one of the most profound artists the world of jazz has ever known.

In the chapter on Louis Armstrong, we learned of his difficult childhood in New Orleans. Billie Holiday suffered an equally troubled upbringing. While Armstrong rose above this beginning, Holiday never did. It continued to undermine her as an adult, resulting in problems with drugs and the law, ultimately leading to her untimely death. Her life paralleled that of bebop legend Charlie Parker in this regard.

Billie Holiday was born Eleanora Fagan in Philadelphia and like Armstrong had an on-again, off-again relationship with her mother. As a teenager, she listened to Armstrong's recordings

Billie Holiday

and to those of blues legend Bessie Smith. Holiday would go on to merge jazz and blues more fully than perhaps any other artist.

Holiday moved as a teenager to New York to be with her mother. Soon, they both landed in jail. After her release, Holiday began singing in clubs around the city and was discovered by record producer John Hammond, who as you'll recall also found Count Basie.

Hammond paired Holiday with yet another discovery, bandmaster Benny Goodman. Her musical association with the King of Swing did not last as long as it did with the pianist she met in Goodman's band, Teddy Wilson.

Holiday and Wilson made an incomparable duo. Fortunately for us, they signed to the Brunswick record label, which gave them the freedom to interpret songs as they wished. Their swinging, improvised renderings of popular standards resulted in a number of late 1930s and early 1940s recordings that would become classics, including "Pennies from Heaven" and "Nice Work if You Can Get It."

Holiday also enjoyed collaborating with tenor saxophonist Lester Young. She had known him she was a teenager, and they had a special rapport with one another. It was Young who gave Holiday her nickname, Lady Day. She, in turn, gave him his, the President, most often shortened to Prez.

Together, Holiday and Young recorded memorable performances of a number of jazz standards, including "The Man I Love" and "Mean to Me." Young's relaxed playing always seemed to bring out the romance in Holiday's interpretations.

MATURE BEYOND HER YEARS

Holiday's status as a singer increased significantly in 1939. It occurred through a song about lynching (illegal hanging),"Strange Fruit." The song's condemnation of racism made it stand out from typical jazz songs and their lighter themes, such as romantic love. Her impassioned performance of its lyrics brought Holiday much acclaim, especially among more liberal members of polite society. With "Strange Fruit," Holiday was embraced as a serious artist like few jazz musicians before her.

It is a said that a person must earn the right to sing the blues. Holiday certainly did so through her troubled existence. Many of her recordings bear the obvious mark of sorrow and weariness. You can hear it clearly in one of her most famous recordings, "God Bless the Child" (1941).

Holiday wrote this autobiographical song with the help of the pianist Arthur Herzog, Jr. after an argument with her mother. It begins with a scriptural paraphrase:

Them that's got shall get
Them that's not shall lose
So the Bible says
And it still is news

Holiday's recording of the song is extremely poignant. Weariness and resignation drip from her phrasing to perfectly underscore the lyrics. Only in the bridge does she seem to protest her fate. The recording sold over a million copies and helped further establish Holiday's popularity as a singer.

It is astonishing to think that Holiday was only 26 years old when she recorded "God Bless the Child." She sings with a maturity that makes it sound as if she's more like 56. Perhaps only the 1960s rock singer Janis Joplin could measure up to Holiday in this way.

LADY DAY'S DECLINE

Billie Holiday would continue to experience trouble and heartache throughout the rest of her life. Despite it all, she continued to enjoy artistic success. In 1948, she performed to a sold-out crowd at Carnegie Hall. In 1956, it was two sold-out performances there. Yet, her assorted troubles took a physical toll. She died in 1959 at the age of 44.

Just two years before her passing, Holiday performed her song "Fine and Mellow" live on national television. The special, *The Sound of Jazz,* brought together dozens of the greatest jazz artists of that time and reunited the singer with Lester Young. It is a legendary performance, with Holiday at her bluesy, world-weary best.

The Legacy of Jazz Singers

No one would dispute that Billie Holiday was a jazz singer. She was in fact one of the greatest jazz singers of all time. Yet, she did not improvise like Ella Fitzgerald or a jazz instrumentalist. Most in the jazz world would agree that a front-line instrumentalist who plays in a jazzy style but does not improvise is not a jazz musician. With singers like Billie Holiday, we seem to find an exception to this general rule.

Not all vocalists who sing in a jazzy style are considered jazz musicians, though. Some of the singers who performed with the big bands during the swing era probably fall short of the mark. It seems to depend on the artistic intent of the vocalist. Billie Holiday's strategy was to sing in a way that matched the spirit of the great jazz musicians she performed with, even if she left the improvising to them.

There is a whole range of other vocalists who may or may not be considered jazz. Some—including Frank Sinatra, Lena Horne, Nat King Cole, Tony Bennett, and Mel Tormé—are very fine artists in their own right. It might be better refer to these singers as jazz stylists—a term that takes nothing away from their craft.

We find an important legacy of jazz vocalists in their influence on singers beyond the tradition. Musicians like Louis Armstrong, Ella Fitzgerald, and Billie Holiday enriched the history of jazz.

Frank Sinatra

At the same time, they inspired many popular singers outside of the jazz mainstream. You can still hear their influence today in the music of an artist like Michael Bublé.

Jose Mangual, Machito, and Carlos Vidal, Glen Island Casino, New York, N.Y., ca. July 1947

LATIN JAZZ

In Chapter 1, we learned about the importance of African music in the formation of jazz. African elements were also extremely influential in the development of music in Latin America—the part of the Western hemisphere where Spanish or Portuguese is the main language. This includes Mexico, the countries of South and Central America, and some of the islands of the Caribbean.

Latin jazz developed with the blending of jazz and music from Latin America. The African heritage they both shared made this possible. In a way, Latin music actually seemed to give back to jazz its full rhythmic potential. This had been denied when African approaches to making music had been taken away from slaves in the United States.

Latin jazz originally came about through the efforts of American jazz artists like Dizzy Gillespie and Stan Kenton, with help from talented Latin musicians to be sure. As Latin jazz developed, it became something all its own. Salsa was one important Latin jazz offshoot. Jazz also had an influence on music in Latin America; in particular, the Brazilian form known as *bossa nova* took its harmonic orientation directly from jazz.

Afro-Cuban Jazz

Nobody ever played like Machito, not even in Cuba.—STEVEN JOSEPH LOZA

The transatlantic slave trade brought millions of Africans to not only the United States but also Latin America. Slave owners in the latter region tended to have a different attitude toward music than here. In the US, we largely suppressed African ways of making music and even banned African instruments. Owners in countries like Brazil and Cuba had a more permissive attitude. As a result, a more direct and obvious African heritage developed and continues in the music of Latin America.

We can hear a clear African influence in the complex, pulsating layers of rhythm found in much Latin American music. Instruments with roots in Africa—including drums like the conga and bongo as well as shakers and the rhythm sticks known as claves—typically combine in an ensemble to perform these rhythms.

The island of Cuba has been home to many forms of music with African roots. In some of them, the overall sound remains distinctly African. In others, African rhythms mix with styles that originated in Spain and Portugal, resulting in the unmistakable sound of Latin music.

Just as swing was sweeping across America in the mid-1930s, another dance music was also gaining popularity. The *rumba* was a Cuban style filled with the type of African rhythms just described. Syncopation brought it to life.

THE GREAT BANDLEADERS

Xavier Cugat (1900–1990), bandleader at the Waldorf Astoria Hotel in New York City, did the most to popularize rumba in the

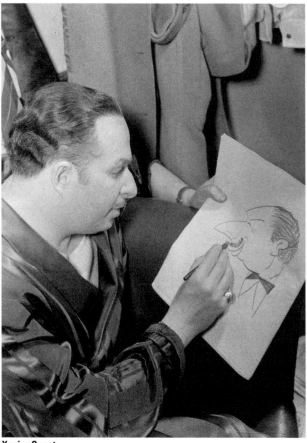

Xavier Cugat

United States. He scored a big hit with his 1935 recording of "El Manicero." With its success, he began appearing on the radio and in Hollywood movies playing music as himself.

Machito (1909–1984) was one of the Cuban musicians who

recorded with Cugat in the United States at the time. He went on to front his own band, the Afro Cubans, in 1940. Machito's ensemble was extremely influential. Mario Bauzá (1911–1993), another Cuban musician living in the United States, scored its arrangements.

Bauzá was also a successful jazz artist. He had already served as lead trumpeter and an arranger for the legendary swing band led by Chick Webb. Bauzá used his experience with swing music in writing for the Afro-Cubans. He combined jazz arrangements and the element of improvisation with Cuban rhythms of African origin. The result of Bauzá's work was something all together different. Latin jazz sprang forth to bring a new rhythmic vibrancy to American music.

A GOOD MARRIAGE

The marriage of jazz and Cuban music seems obvious. Both bear the mark of Africa in their polyrhythms and syncopations. In jazz, though, the influence is less overt since plantation owners in the United States tried to eradicate African influences, including musical ones, among their slaves.

In Cuban music, the African roots of the music are much more obvious. With Latin jazz, we hear how jazz might have developed on its own if a heritage of African music had remained unsuppressed here.

Latin jazz incorporated another element that reveals its origins, one less African. The chord progressions found in much Latin music are quite different from those in the folk and popular music of the United States.

These chord progressions find their origins in Spanish guitar playing, which in turn was influenced by the music of North

Africa. It requires training in music theory to fully understand these progressions, but they sound distinctly Latin to almost everyone.

Getting Dizzy

I don't care much about music. What I like is sounds. —DIZZY GILLESPIE

Mario Bauzá had developed a close relationship with a fellow trumpet player active in New York during the late 1930s. We have already discussed the importance of Dizzy Gillespie in the invention of bebop. Through his association with Machito and Bauzá, he would have a large influence on the development of Latin jazz.

Latin jazz began to hit its full stride when another Cuban musician, the percussionist Chano Pozo (1915–1948), joined Dizzy Gillespie's band, in 1947. While Pozo would die just a year later, he and Gillespie mined rich ore from mixing Latin rhythms with bebop to create a style some have called *cubop.* Other bebop musicians, including Charlie Parker with his 1948 and 1952 Latin recordings on Verve compiled in *South of the Border*, also began dipping their toes into the waters of Cuban rhythm.

MANTECA

The Pozo/Gillespie pairing resulted in the monumental recording of a composition they co-wrote, "Manteca." It begins with Pozo on congas knocking out a hot Cuban rhythm, accompanied only by string bass. After a couple of measures, baritone saxophonist Cecil Payne enters. Rather than playing a melody, he plays a syncopated rhythm that adds another polyrhythmic layer.

Brass instruments soon join in, playing more syncopated rhythms rather than melodies. Dizzy begins improvising fiery, molten licks over this rhythmic foundation. In the next section, saxophones and brass battle against one another. There is still no

Dizzy Gillespie

melody to speak of. The performance is all about groove.

What most of us would identify as a melody does not enter until a minute into the recording. It is a smooth, lyrical line played by saxophones. Dizzy follows this with his own melodic line, but it soon gives way to a return to the ensemble laying down layers of rhythm. The horns drop out soon enough, and we are left with just congas and bass again.

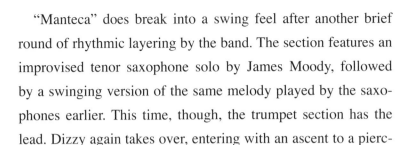

"Manteca" does break into a swing feel after another brief round of rhythmic layering by the band. The section features an improvised tenor saxophone solo by James Moody, followed by a swinging version of the same melody played by the saxophones earlier. This time, though, the trumpet section has the lead. Dizzy again takes over, entering with an ascent to a piercing high E♭. The band brings the song to a close with more layering of rhythms that again give way to just congas and bass.

Gillespie cheerfully shouts out, "Manteca, Manteca!" at the end of the recording and several points earlier in the piece. Dizzy got his nickname through his sense of humor, and it seems to show here. *Manteca* is simply the Spanish word for lard.

OTHER CUBAN ELEMENTS

Dizzy Gillespie would continue to incorporate Cuban elements into his music during the rest of his long career. In fact, when it was no longer possible for him to blow the trumpet as well as he once had, he turned to playing the conga.

Other jazz musicians followed in their own pursuit of Cuban rhythms. The big band leader Stan Kenton played an especially important role in furthering Latin jazz. Other Cuban styles would come along to keep the musical fires stoked; Cuban musicians like Ramón "Mongo" Santamaría and Israel "Cachao" López partnered with American jazz artists such as trumpeters Jon Faddis and Lew Soloff.

Brazilian Jazz

The music that developed in the South American country of Brazil bears some similarity to the music of Cuba. Both Brazil and Cuba were slave-owning Latin colonies of the New World. It is little wonder then that we find layers of African-derived rhythms in Brazil, just as we do in Cuba. Beyond this though, Cuban and Brazilian music are quite distinct from one another.

Geographically, Brazil is much farther from the United States than Cuba or Puerto Rico. There are also far fewer emigrants from Brazil than from the Caribbean living in America. Nonetheless, a musical import from Brazil achieved widespread popularity in the United States for a few years in the 1960s. It continues to inspire jazz musicians to this day.

Bossa nova means "new trend" in Portuguese. The "old trend" was the *samba*, the national dance music of Brazil. Compared to samba, bossa nova was much more relaxed and featured a characteristic swaying rhythm. It also incorporated some international elements. In particular, bossa nova relied on the type of sophisticated harmonies heard in modern jazz.

Bossa nova did not depart entirely from the samba. It took from the older music an emphasis on the second beat of the four-beat measure. It also borrowed syncopation, a characteristic that reveals its African heritage.

LIVES AND TIMES

Colonization The discovery of the New World by Christopher Columbus in 1492 resulted in the colonization of all of Latin America and the Caribbean, mainly by Spain and Portugal. This resulted in the development of Latin culture. The importation of slaves added African elements to it, and the intermingling of Latin, African, and native cultures continues to this day.

Panama Canal The United States completed a canal linking the Atlantic and Pacific Oceans in 1914. It greatly facilitated the worldwide shipping of cargo and brought political changes to the region. The Panama Canal also focused American attention on Latin America.

Cuban Revolution When communist rebels under Fidel Castro came to power in Cuba, in 1959, it led to a cutting of ties with the United States. Before the revolution, there had been a free-flowing relationship between the two. One of its products was the creation of Latin jazz.

THE BIRTH OF BOSSA NOVA

The samba developed in the shantytowns of Rio de Janeiro at the beginning of the 20th century. Bossa nova came more from the clubs and resorts along the city's Copacabana beach during the

1950s. It was the invention of a handful of Brazilian composers, principally João Gilberto, Alfredo Jos da Silva, and Antonio Carlos Jobim.

Bossa nova came to prominence in 1958 with the release of Gilberto's "Bim-Bom" and his recording of Jobim's "Chega de Saudade." Gilberto's nylon-string guitar playing and the relaxed, unadorned singing of Elizete Cardoso as well as Gilberto himself became closely associated with the emerging style.

The American jazz guitarist Charlie Byrd (1925–1999) receives the most credit for importing bossa nova to the United States. Byrd took part in a musical State Department tour of Latin America in 1961 and brought back with him recordings by Gilberto and Jobim, which he then played for tenor saxophonist Stan Getz. This proved to be a key moment in jazz history.

Byrd and Getz decided they wanted to try blending bossa nova with jazz. It seemed like an obvious pairing. After all, jazz had harmonically inspired bossa nova, and the relaxed sound of the Brazilian music was reminiscent of cool jazz.

After a few halting attempts, Byrd and Getz succeeded in creating the musical hybrid they sought. It appeared on an album *Jazz Samba*, which reached #1 on the American pop charts in 1963.

THE GIRL FROM IPANEMA

The success of *Jazz Samba* helped create a worldwide craze for bossa nova. Getz followed up with several more albums inspired by the music of Brazil. 1964's *Getz/Gilberto* became one of the best selling jazz albums of all time. It included a song that would quickly become a jazz standard, "The Girl from Ipanema."

Antonio Carlos Jobim wrote the music for "The Girl from

Ipanema." The Getz/Gilberto recording begins with just João Gilberto, who sings the Portuguese lyrics in a wonderfully off-hand way, accompanying himself with syncopated chords on nylon-string guitar. Percussion softly enters along with gentle lines played by the piano at the repeat of the bridge.

Gilberto's wife, Astrud, takes over the vocal on the second go-round. This time it is in English, and she continues in the same relaxed, unaffected way as her husband. The recording

launched an international career for Astrud. Her voice would become *the* voice of bossa nova.

Getz does not enter until the second repeat of the melody. His saxophone performance begins in a subdued way as well. His breathy tone, a Getz trademark, is obvious. It somehow lends a great deal to the laidback yet sultry feel of the performance. The listener can easily imagine a ceiling fan slowly turning in an open cabana on a Rio beach.

Getz's entrance may be muted but with it the rhythm section becomes more energetic and jazzy. As his performance continues, the ensemble opens up and Getz begins to improvise around the melody. There is a distinct playfulness to the liberties he takes with the return of the main melody after the bridge.

Getz next hands over the song to its composer on piano. The voicings that Jobim uses to harmonize the melody make obvious the affinity between bossa nova and jazz. Astrud enters again at the bridge, this time accompanied by Getz. She calls with the melody, and Getz responds with improvised phrases. Their sounds blend beautifully, like two perfectly matched pastel colors.

The success of *Jazz Samba* and *Getz/Gilberto* created an appetite for Brazilian rhythms that helped rekindle interest in jazz.

On the whole, the music had suffered commercially ever since rock 'n' roll toke over the airwaves in the 1950s. The United States was experiencing a baby boom and the elemental sounds of rock were more appealing to American teenagers than jazz.

The problem for the Brazilian jazz movement turned out to be the same thing that had helped make it so popular—its relaxed sound. It made soothing background music for dentist offices and elevators, becoming a stereotype that proved impossible for the style to shake.

Beyond Cuba and Brazil

If there is no dance, there is not music.
—TITO PUENTE

While technically not Latin jazz, the music of the Belgian guitarist Jean "Django" Reinhardt (1910–1953) has a broad relationship with it. Reinhardt was a Romani gypsy, and the music of the Romani both influenced Spanish music and was influenced by it. We can hear echoes of gypsy music in much of Reinhardt's playing. It is particularly clear in his recording of "Minor Swing." For this reason, Django's music is often called gypsy jazz or gypsy swing.

Reinhardt found a musical home in France. There, he and French violinist Stéphane Grappelli (1908–1997) formed a legendary small jazz ensemble in 1934, Quintette du Hot Club de France. It reemerged after the devastation of World War II. Together, the pair helped establish an important European strain of jazz, one with gypsy overtones.

Gypsy jazz continues in various forms to this day in France and beyond. The annual Festival de Jazz Django Reinhardt in

Samois-sur-Seine, France helps support it. Two of the best per-formers today are the gypsy guitarists Stochelo Rosenberg and Biréli Lagrène. You can hear obvious but updated echoes of Re-inhardt in the playing of both.

RUMBA, MAMBO, AND SON

The rhythms of Cuban music fueled the initial development of Latin jazz in the 1940s. A decade later a new Cuban dance came along to refuel the movement. Like the rumba, the *mambo* fused together European and African elements. Howev-er, the underlying rhythm is subtly different.

SUGGESTED LISTENING

DIZZY GILLESPIE
"Cubana Be, Cubana Bop"
"Jungla"
"Manteca"

DJANGO REINHARDT
"Brazil"
"Honeysuckle Rose"
"Minor Swing"

STAN GETZ
"Con Alma"
"Desafinado"
"The Girl from Ipanema"

TITO PUENTE
"Mambo Gozon"
"Oye Como Va"
"Ran Kan Kan"

Cuban bandmaster Pérez Prado moved to Mexico City in 1948 and then on to New York seeking musical success. He brought with him fiery arrangements and the mambo's propul-sive beat. In large part through Prado's efforts, the United States developed a large appetite for mam-bos by the mid-1950s. Even American pop singer Perry Como got into the act with his recording of "Papa Loves Mambo."

The rumba and mambo made a return trip to Cuba in the 1940s and 1950s as Latin jazz. The hybrid was particularly popular in the nightclubs that attracted tourists from the United States. There, it began to blend with other native music like the cha-cha-cha.

Son was one of the Cuban styles to mingle with Latin jazz during this period. Small groups originally accompanied the son dance. Their instruments included the Cuban guitar, the *tres*, as well Latin percussion instruments like the claves, maracas, and bongos. By the 1950s, son ensembles had grown to include wind instruments, piano, and bass. This helped infuse with Latin jazz.

PUERTO RICAN SOUNDS

Puerto Rico lies just east of Cuba. Both Caribbean islands were originally slave-owning colonies of Spain. Not surprisingly, we find African-derived rhythms mixed with Spanish styles in the music of both islands.

As an American territory, Puerto Rico has had an especially close relationship with the mainland of the United States. This has resulted in a large Puerto Rican population in New York and other American cities. With it has come a large market for Latin music and opportunities for musicians with Puerto Rican roots.

A child of Puerto Rican immigrants, Tito Puente (1920–2000) became one of the most important American mambo artists of the 1950s. As other Latin styles like the son came along, he added them to his band's repertoire. Puente was an accomplished timbales player and reigned for decades as the King of Latin Music.

Over time, the various styles of Cuban music and Latin jazz merged into what is now modern salsa. Even though Puente disliked the term salsa, he became its most recognizable artist. Not only did he bring the music to the mainstream in the United States, he helped spread it throughout Latin America.

The Legacy of Latin Jazz

Latin jazz enjoys a number of legacies. First, it established new rhythmic potential for jazz beyond swing. Swing remains the default rhythmic feel for jazz, but Latin music brought to it other possibilities. Even today, many jazz musicians include some Latin tunes in performances and on recordings.

Stan Getz

Latin rhythm also provided jazz with an international passport, allowing the music to journey south and speak the musical language of Cuba and Brazil. When infused with Latin rhythms, jazz became less foreign in such countries. This encouraged further musical development in Latin American, as we saw with both the bossa nova and the son.

The work of Dizzy Gillespie, Stan Getz, Tito Puente, and

others also showed that jazz could be successfully grafted with other musical styles. Latin jazz became the genre's first fusion music. Other successful blends would come along, especially that of rock and jazz as well as funk and jazz, but Latin jazz was the first.

Finally, what started with the mixing of jazz and Cuban rhythms has grown into its own musical forms. For example, while jazz and salsa artists share a musical bond, they now come from two different worlds. This is perhaps the greatest legacy of Latin jazz. It has helped give birth to musical styles that have grown beyond it to have their own musical identities.

Dave Brubeck

COOL JAZZ
AND BEYOND

Traditional jazz was hot music. This was true for both the early jazz of New Orleans and its child, the jazz of 1920s Chicago. Louis Armstrong even called his Chicago bands the Hot Five and Hot Seven. In Europe, they referred to it as *le jazz hot*. The association of traditional jazz with heat becomes clear when you listen to the blazing solos and fiery tempos of the music.

Swing music lowered the overall temperature of jazz a little in the 1930s. However, the bebop revolution brought the heat back up to a feverish degree. Listen to recordings of artists like Charlie Parker and Dizzy Gillespie and you hear *le jazz scorching hot*.

With bebop, some thought jazz had actually started to boil over. A counterrevolution developed in the late 1940s. A number of artists who had helped establish bebop led the charge, particularly Miles Davis. The insurrection also involved musicians from beyond the jazz mainstream. A number came from California. They brought with them a more relaxed approach to music.

The musical movement came to be known as cool jazz. As the name suggests, it featured relaxed tempos and a laidback approach to performing. It also incorporated influences from classical music, including a few orchestral instruments.

Birth of the Cool

Hot can be cool and cool can be hot and each can be both. But hot or cool, man, jazz is jazz.—LOUIS ARMSTRONG

The saxophonist Lester Young, whom we've encountered in previous chapters, stands as a major figure in the history of jazz. He was a towering presence in Count Basie's band and also helped inspire the development of bebop. Fellow jazz musicians prized his recordings with Billie Holiday.

Young became known for the sophisticated harmonic ideas he brought to his improvisations. What set him apart most, though, was the relaxed, smooth tone he produced on tenor saxophone. You can hear it clearly in his 1938 recording with Billie Holiday of "I Can't Get Started." Prez, as Holiday dubbed him, was cool long before it was cool to be cool.

The music of conservatory-educated Claude Thornhill also inspired the development of cool jazz. He encouraged the musicians in his swing band to play without vibrato. This lent a subdued sound to the arrangements they played. That and Thornhill's soft, tinkling piano lend a wonderful chill to his best-known work, "Snowfall" (1941). Thornhill's arranger Gil Evans remembers, "The sound hung like a cloud."

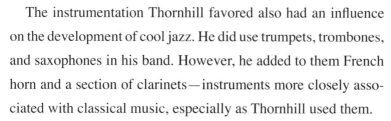

The instrumentation Thornhill favored also had an influence on the development of cool jazz. He did use trumpets, trombones, and saxophones in his band. However, he added to them French horn and a section of clarinets—instruments more closely associated with classical music, especially as Thornhill used them.

After serving in the military during World War II, Thornhill put together a new band. It featured young musicians who would become driving forces in the cool jazz movement, including saxophonists Lee Konitz and Gerry Mulligan. Mulligan also served as an arranger for Thornhill.

GIL EVANS AND MILES DAVIS

Gil Evans (1912–1988) spent most of his youth growing up in California. In the early 1940s, he moved to New York City, where his apartment became a hangout for progressive jazz musicians. In 1948, he joined forces with former Thornhill alumnus Mulligan to create compositions for a new *nonet* (nine-member ensemble) led by Miles Davis.

The dozen works recorded in 1949 and 1950 by this group would eventually appear as *Birth of the Cool*—one of the most apt titles in jazz history, as well as one of the most important albums.

Birth of the Cool builds upon the musical approach pioneered by Thornhill. It is there in the Thornhill-like instrumentation, which includes French horn and tuba. It is also there in the simple textures and lack of vibrato. Yet, there is also something new. We hear the birth of a new style that Thornhill only helped father.

Almost every composition found on *Birth of the Cool* shines like a gemstone. Some are cooler than others, though. "Budo" and "Move" cook away at bebop-approved tempos and display

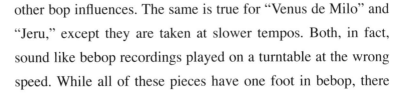

other bop influences. The same is true for "Venus de Milo" and "Jeru," except they are taken at slower tempos. Both, in fact, sound like bebop recordings played on a turntable at the wrong speed. While all of these pieces have one foot in bebop, there is still something understated about them. An obvious coolness pervades the arrangements.

LIVES AND TIMES

Cold War The United States and the Soviet Union emerged form World War II as the two great victors. They held radically different worldviews and large nuclear arsenals by the 1950s. This led to a political and military stalemate that shaped much of history for several decades.

Suburbia Americans enjoyed great prosperity following World War II. Many citizens built dream houses in newly created suburbs on the outskirts of cities. A suburban way of living developed, becoming the American dream during the 1950s.

Television A new technology became common in living rooms in suburban America during the 1950s. Radio had brought the sounds of news and entertainment into homes a few decades before. Television now added a visual element. It quickly became a major source of entertainment that helped spread a range of ideas.

BOPLICITY

"Boplicity" is perhaps the coolest of all the works recorded by the Miles Davis nonet. Composed by Davis and arranged by Gil Evans, the piece swings with low-key sophistication. No introduction is needed. All of the horns enter together.

The trumpet carries the melody at the beginning of "Boplicity," while the other winds shadow it. Together, they create a tight cluster of sound. The melody contains the type of syncopation and scalar jumps heard in bebop. There are also cool gestures, like the lazy triplet heard in the second measure.

The rhythm section simply consists of drums using brushes and a bass walking a simple line. The piano does not enter until Gerry Mulligan plays the first improvised solo. He plays baritone saxophone and avoids the honky sound commonly associated with the instrument.

At the end of Mulligan's solo, the wind instruments briefly reenter. They coil around each other polyphonically, playing a number of musical lines at the same time. Polyphony is also

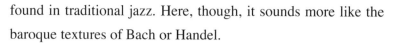

found in traditional jazz. Here, though, it sounds more like the baroque textures of Bach or Handel.

About a minute and a half into the recording, Davis briefly enters with his own solo. Other instruments soon join him to play harmony lines that sound improvised but are not. Near the end of the section, the tuba plays a separate part, again creating a polyphonic texture.

At this point, "Boplicity" becomes more conventional. Davis continues to improvise. He swings away and the rest of the wind instruments play a backing melody. Evans then takes over to improvise on piano.

Neither Evans nor any of the other improvisers breaks into double time as they might with bebop. Everyone keeps things cool. "Boplicity" ends with the ensemble again playing the melody heard at the top of the piece.

BEYOND BIRTH OF THE COOL

The nonet heard on the *Birth of the Cool* sessions performed live now and then for a couple years. Although Miles Davis served as its leader, it did not meet with much success. Perhaps the music was simply ahead of its time. After all, bebop was still going strong and had not been around that long itself.

The group's interracial makeup was also criticized. A good deal of the criticism came from black musicians who did not appreciate the inclusion of white performers. Davis rejected their concerns and was frustrated by the ensemble's relative failure.

The musicians associated with *Birth of the Cool* would go on to follow different paths. Davis pioneered other styles of jazz in the 1950s and beyond, as you'll learn in the next chapter. Gil Evans teamed up with Davis again to produce several landmark albums a decade later, including *Porgy and Bess* (1958) and *Sketches of Spain* (1960). Another Thornhill alumnus, alto saxophonist Lee Konitz, continued as a leading figure of cool jazz. He seemed to shine brightest in collaborative efforts, as heard on the albums *Lee Konitz with Warne Marsh* (1955) and *The Lee Konitz Duets* (1967).

The *Birth of the Cool* recordings inspired a range of jazz artists. One was pianist Lennie Tristano, who served as collaborator with and mentor to Konitz. Deeply innovative, Tristano helped expand jazz's harmonic palette and even experimented with recording effects like overdubbing and tape-speed manipulation. He is also remembered as an important jazz educator.

The members of the Modern Jazz Quartet also found inspiration in cool jazz. The MJQ was a renowned and long-lived ensemble that took the cool style in its own direction, blending it with other musical elements to create a distinct sound. In particular, the members had a wonderful knack for group improvisation. Their impromptu flights created polyphonic lines that remind the listeners as much of baroque music as traditional jazz.

West Coast Jazz

You can be better than your technique.
You can be better than most of your usual
ideas. —DAVE BRUBECK

While New York gave birth to cool jazz, it did not find its true home there. By the mid-1950s, the city was starting to resound more with the strains of hard bop. This developed in part as a backlash against what were seen as the non-jazz elements in cool music—interesting since hard bop itself mixed bebop with out-

side forms, like rhythm and blues and gospel.

A city on the opposite side of the country adopted the orphaned cool jazz. Los Angeles was enjoying a postwar economic boom in the 1950s. The Los Angeles music scene was also quickly emerging as a dominant force. It took the cool style and developed it into what became known as West Coast jazz.

MULLIGAN AND BAKER

Not all of the musicians associated with West Coast jazz were from Los Angeles. Gerry Mulligan, who first made a name for himself in New York, moved to Los Angeles in 1952. There, he started arranging for the big band led by Stan Kenton. He also began playing in a quartet at a local club with a young trumpeter and vocalist from Oklahoma, Chet Baker. This piano-less group packed in the crowds and found instant success on record.

We can hear why the Mulligan and Baker quartet was so popular by listening to its recording of the Mul-ligan composition "Walkin' Shoes." "Ambling Shoes" might be a better title since the piece sashays along at such a cool, leisurely stride. The melody glides above drummer Chico Hamilton on brushes and bassist Bob Whitlock playing an easy walking line.

Mulligan and Baker both play the melody for "Walkin' Shoes" in a restrained manner without even a hint of vibrato. They are in unison for the most part but occasionally break into harmony. After the melody, Mulligan takes a solo. Next comes Baker. Behind him Mulligan plays a simple background line to create a counterpoint between the two—a signature trait for Mulligan and Baker.

Gerry Mulligan

The pairing of Mulligan and Baker only lasted until 1953. Mulligan would go on to perform and record with many other jazz artists. He also composed and commissioned a number of chamber and orchestral works that took jazz beyond its natural habitat. Baker's career was hindered by drug problems and prison stays. Later in life, he enjoyed a musical comeback, especially in Europe.

DAVE BRUBECK

Cool jazz also found a West Coast home in San Francisco, where pianist Dave Brubeck and alto saxophonist Paul Desmond formed a quartet that would lead the style in a different direction. The son of a Californian rancher, Brubeck took piano lessons as a child from his mother, who was classically trained and had wanted to become a concert pianist.

These classical leanings rubbed off on Brubeck. As a young man, he studied music at the College of the Pacific. He was then drafted into the army during World War II and headed up one of the military's first integrated bands. After release, he studied composition under Darius Milhaud at Mills College. He even took a couple of lessons with the legendary modern composer Arnold Schoenberg, who was then teaching at UCLA.

Brubeck clearly held artistic goals beyond jazz. They appear a little in the first recording by the Brubeck/Desmond quartet, *Jazz Goes to College* (1954). The album is mainly cool jazz, though. You can hear its strains most clearly in Desmond's wispy tone and understated phrasing. Even when the tempo heats up on some tunes, Desmond remains cool, calm, and collected.

Jazz Goes to College enjoyed great commercial success and even landed Brubeck on the cover of *Time* magazine. He was only the second jazz artist to be honored in this way. The first, as you'll remember, was Louis Armstrong. The title of the album came from the quartet's appearances at American universities and colleges. This was something new. Now, there are plenty of degree programs in jazz, but back then, the music was generally considered unfit for college students.

The Dave Brubeck Quartet remained successful through the remainder of the 1950s. Drummer Joe Morello joined the group in 1956. A classically trained musician like Brubeck, he brought his own distinctive style to the ensemble. The addition of bassist Eugene Wright in 1958 made the otherwise white quartet inter-racial.

A racially mixed ensemble was still unusual at the time. Brubeck was committed to racial equality, though, and turned down performances and even a television appearance that would not accept Wright.

In 1959, the Dave Brubeck Quartet released its landmark al-bum *Time Out*. The product of a musical experiment, it featured compositions in unusual time signatures. One of the best-known pieces from the album is "Blue Rondo à la Turk." Its melody begins with nine beats per measure, subdivided 2, 2, 2, 3. Such odd meters lent an exotic and modern feel to the album.

TAKE FIVE

The hit single from *Time Out* was Paul Desmond's "Take Five." The piece's catchy melody and understated saxophone perfor-mance helped it place high on the *Billboard* charts. There was also something captivating about the "Take Five" rhythm. Its five-beat measures set heads bobbing and feet tapping in a new way.

Joe Morello starts out "Take Five" lightly, playing a ride pat-tern on cymbal and a syncopated phrase on snare drum. Piano followed by bass softly complement this when they enter one after the other. Together, the rhythm section lays down the song's signature groove, which swings along in a three-plus-two beat pattern, with emphasis on beat 1 of each measure.

The rhythm section continues this groove when Desmond en-ters with the melody. His playing is casual and unhurried; his airy tone, intimate but cool. During the bridge, the melody becomes more animated. It dances in an easygoing, lighthearted way and seems to skip down a sun-dappled street. The return of the main melody brings with it a return of the original coolness.

Desmond easily glides out of the melody and into his improvisation, which is also relaxed and understated. Behind him, the rhythm section simply repeats the phrase that serves as the main riff for "Take Five." Many of Desmond's lines join with the rhythm section to emphasize beat 1. At times, there is also a bluesy tinge to his playing.

After Desmond drops out, Morello solos on drums. The fact that this is a solo is not immediately obvious since he continues laying down the main groove with piano and bass. The ensemble builds in intensity and Morello gradually breaks away from them. Eventually, piano and bass are left repeating the same phrase as the drums add loud exclamations on snare, bass, and tom-tom.

Morello's solo lasts for nearly two and half minutes—almost half the length of the entire recording. It is one of the most famous drum solos in jazz history, but not because it is flashy.

Morello himself commented, "When people use the word 'technique,' they usually mean 'speed.' But the solo had very little speed involved. It was more about space and playing over the bar line. It was conspicuous by being so different." In the true spirit of coolness, Morello showed that less can be more.

"Take Five" ends with a return to the head. The ensemble plays it straight through, including the dancing bridge. Desmond repeats the last measure of the main melody several times as a coda. The band ends together on the first beat of the measure with Morello's ride cymbal continuing to ring out.

Classical and Jazz

Classical music and jazz might seem worlds apart in many ways. Performing the great works of master composers leaves little room for spontaneous expression. On the other, such expression is the very heart of jazz. Despite the difference, jazz has occasionally inspired the classical world. For example, jazzy strains enliven Stravinsky's *Ebony Concerto* and Aaron Copland's *Music from the Theater.*

Dave Brubeck's composition teacher, Darius Milhaud, was one of the earliest classical adopters of jazz. During a 1922 trip to the United States, the Frenchman heard the music performed live. Returning to Europe, he penned his ballet *La création du monde.* Critics of the time scoffed at its bluesy turns and jazzy rhythms, but it has gone on to become a staple in the concert world.

Classical music has also had its influence on jazz. Tin Pan Alley composer George Gershwin composed *Rhapsody in Blue* in 1924 for solo piano and jazz band. The Paul Whiteman orchestra even debuted it with the composer on piano. Duke Ellington often showed classical leanings, as well.

Above, we learned that the compositions recorded during The *Birth of the Cool* sessions displayed their own classical elements. In particular, the use of French horn and tuba helped create something of a chamber ensemble. Compositional techniques like counterpoint also contributed to a classical air.

Dave Brubeck blended jazz with classical elements in his own way. It is said that his improvisations threw in "a little canon a la Bach or some dissonant counterpoint a la Bartok or even a thrashing crisis a la Beethoven." Milhaud must have been proud of his pupil.

THE THIRD STREAM

The classical leanings of the cool movement helped the development of a new musical genre. Third stream music sits halfway between the classical world and jazz. Composer Gunther Schuller coined the term in 1957. His works also helped define it. His *Concertino* (1959) features a jazz quartet with orchestra and *Variants on a Theme of Thelonious Monk* (1960) was recorded by some of the best progressive jazz musicians of the day, including saxophonists Ornette Coleman, Eric Dolphy, and pianist Bill Evans. An important educator, Schuller also established what is now the New England Conservatory's Contemporary Improvisation program, now directed by pianist Ran Blake.

Other composers helped develop third stream music. Pianist John Lewis, who was closely associated with Schuller, and his Modern Jazz Quartet played an important role. Trumpeter Don Ellis was also inspired by the trend. Early in his career, he worked with both Schuller and composer/conductor Leonard Bernstein on third stream projects. He later went on to form his own band and write compositions that blended jazz with classical elements.

SUGGESTED LISTENING

DAVE BRUBECK
"Blue Rondo à la Turk."
"Take Five"

ORNETTE COLEMAN
"Free Jazz"

MILES DAVIS
"Boplicity"
"Jeru"
"Rocker"

CHARLES MINGUS
"Mode D–Trio and Group Dancers"
"Haitian Fight Song"

GERRY MULLIGAN
"Bernie's Tune"
"Walkin' Shoes"

CECIL TAYLOR
"Enter, Evening"

Charles Mingus

Charles Mingus is also sometimes cited as a third-stream artist. His important contributions to jazz were farther ranging than any one movement or style, though. On the one hand, much of Mingus' music drew from the soulful rhythms of hard bop. On the other, he also emphasized the collective improvisation that was a hallmark of the traditional jazz that came from New Orleans. And these were just two facets of a musical style that was

Charles Mingus

extraordinarily multifaceted.

Mingus is remembered both for his brilliance on the bass and as a composer with the sort of serious artistic intent held by Duke Ellington. His 1963 album *The Black Saint and the Sinner Lady*

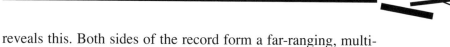

reveals this. Both sides of the record form a far-ranging, multi-movement work that was partly conceived as a ballet. Mingus referred to the music recorded for the album by an 11-piece ensemble as "ethnic folk-dance music."

FREE JAZZ

Mingus also took part in a musical movement that eclipsed third stream music to certain extent in the 1960s. The improvisatory liberty of free jazz captured the imagination of some leading jazz figures, seemingly drawing interest away from third stream. Perhaps because of this, the third stream movement never developed as fully as it might have.

Many critics decried free jazz as musical anarchy. Even Mingus initially was not impressed. "If the free-form guys could play the same tune twice, then I would say they were playing something," he said. Still, free jazz represented an artistic liberty that some found compelling, and Mingus soon enough joined them in this assessment.

A change in musical style underlies many of the revolutions in the history of jazz, including swing, bebop, and Latin jazz. Free jazz, though, constituted a break from style all together, and it is better to refer to it as a musical approach. It intentionally broke down such conventions of jazz as set melody and harmonic progression, tempo, rhythmic groove, and the like. Some free jazz musicians even saw the term jazz as limiting and did not want it attached to their efforts.

Since many of those involved in the free jazz movement came from a jazz background, they brought with them the jazz orientation of the music. Their performances actually distilled and emphasized the spontaneity and collective creativity that had been hallmarks of jazz since its days in the Storyville section of New Orleans. Other aspects of the jazz tradition, including swing rhythms and harmonic structures, also bubble to the surface in many free improvisations.

ORNETTE COLEMAN, CECIL TAYLOR, AND OTHERS

Saxophonist Ornette Coleman and pianist Cecil Taylor did much to pioneer the free jazz approach. Coleman's raw and vocal playing revealed blues tinges and often sought notes in between the standard pitches.

For his part, Taylor seemed to treat the piano more as a drum than a melodic or harmonic instrument, his playing was filled with tight clusters of notes and polyrhythms.

Coleman's 1960 album *Free Jazz: A Collective Improvisation* marks a watershed moment in the development of the music. Its title even stands as something of a dictionary entry for the approach. The recording features two quartets, one for each channel of the stereo mix, that sometimes seem to musically battle one another. It is aggressive music set against a fast, swinging rhythm.

Other musicians to explore the artistic possibilities of free jazz in the 1960s and beyond included saxophonists Pharoah Sanders, Sun Ra, and Eric Dolphy—who also played other woodwind instruments, like the bass clarinet. John Coltrane, profiled in the next chapter, also found inspiration in free jazz. His 1966 album *Ascension* was in fact a landmark work in the free-jazz movement.

Free jazz helped inspire the loft jazz scene of the 1970s, where musicians played in large, open spaces of former industrial buildings in New York City. Saxophonist Anthony Braxton and members of the Association for the Advancement of Creative Musicians (AACM) were known for their involvement on

Ornette Coleman

that scene. Artists like guitarist James (Blood) Ulmer also began experimenting with freer versions of fusion.

Fast forwarding to the 21st century, with the music of saxophonist John Zorn we can hear bold experiments with roots in free jazz, as well as in many other idioms including contemporary classical and even hardcore.

The Legacy of Cool Jazz and Other Styles

Some stylistic developments in the history of jazz became mainstream movements. In doing so, they largely replaced what had come before. Swing took the place of traditional jazz, bebop took the place of swing, and so on. That was not true for cool jazz. It did not replace anything but instead served as an alternative.

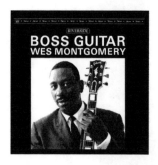

The cool jazz movement did not last for long. It emerged at the end of the 1940s and reached a peak in the early 1950s. By the early 1960s cool jazz was largely a thing of the past. Dave Brubeck was the one great exception.

Cool jazz did create a larger legacy. While it may have been short-lived itself, it did bequeath a relaxed, understated approach to other styles. One example is the bossa nova that developed in Brazil during the 1950s; another is the fusing of bossa nova with jazz that led by saxophonist Stan Getz in the 1960s. Both bear the clear mark of cool jazz.

Today's smooth jazz also owes much to the cool movement. This style dates from the late 1960s and the work of guitarist Wes Montgomery. In the 1970s, musicians like Earl Klugh and George Benson (who both happen to also be guitarists) developed smooth jazz into a style that reigns on light radio stations to this day. While it incorporates influences from pop, R&B, and other musical genres, its debt to cool jazz is undeniable.

Another movement, free jazz, developed out of frustration with the limitations of cool jazz and other styles that had fixed

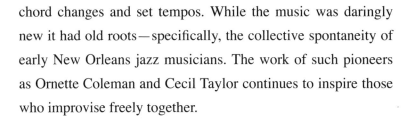

chord changes and set tempos. While the music was daringly new it had old roots—specifically, the collective spontaneity of early New Orleans jazz musicians. The work of such pioneers as Ornette Coleman and Cecil Taylor continues to inspire those who improvise freely together.

John Coltrane and Miles Davis

MILES AND COLTRANE

If there ever were a Mount Rushmore of jazz, it would certainly have to feature Louis Armstrong. It would also no doubt include Duke Ellington and Charlie Parker. Lovers of jazz would have a lively debate about other worthy figures, though. Ella Fitzgerald? Billie Holiday? This chapter looks at two jazz greats who many believe deserve to be immortalized in such a way: Miles Davis and John Coltrane.

Of the pair, Miles Davis (1926–1991) has had the broadest influence on jazz. He started out as young bebop musician playing on the bandstand with Charlie Parker. He then emerged as a leader of the cool jazz movement. Never one to rest on his achievements, Davis went on to serve as a leading light in the hard bop, modal jazz and fusion movements. Near the end of his life, Davis was even blending jazz with hip-hop.

The career of John Coltrane (1926–1967) was shorter. Coltrane rose in the world of jazz as a member of combos led by Davis. He then became a leader of his own groups for a few years. During this latter period, Coltrane mainly pursued modal and free jazz. He did so with such musical brilliance that he stands as one of the most revered jazz artists of all time.

Miles Ahead

I know what I've done for music, but don't call me a legend. Just call me Miles Davis.—
MILES DAVIS

Miles Davis grew up in a stable middle-class home in East St. Louis, Illinois. The son of a dentist, he began playing music at 13 when his father gave him a trumpet. Miles took lessons and was playing professionally with local groups just a couple of years later. A band passing through town tried to get him to join their group, but Davis' mother insisted that he finish high school.

A key event took place just after Davis graduated. The Billy Eckstine Big Band played an extended engagement in St. Louis. The ensemble featured Charlie Parker and Dizzy Gillespie, two of the leading figures in the development of bebop. When one of Eckstine's other musicians fell ill, Miles received the opportunity to substitute for him.

Inspired by Parker and Gillespie, Davis soon moved to New York and enrolled in what would become the Juilliard School of Music. He did not particularly enjoy his classes there. Davis felt they concentrated too much on classical music, but he did appreciate the music theory he learned. Besides, he wanted to be a jazz musician. He was busy seeking out the artists who inspired him, especially Charlie Parker.

BEBOP SESSIONS

Miles soon found himself playing jam sessions at Minton's Playhouse. A hotbed for the emerging bebop revolution, the club attracted Parker and Gillespie as well as other bebop pioneers, like Thelonious Monk and Kenny Clarke. For Davis, Minton's bandstand was his real classroom.

In 1945, Gillespie left Parker's quintet and the saxophonist hired Davis to replace him. Miles had made a few recordings prior to this. However, his records with Parker are what begin to show us the type of musician he would become. In them, we typically hear Parker darting about at high speed during his solos. Meanwhile, Davis plays in a much more melodic and relaxed manner. The contrast between them is striking.

Parker's group faced challenges. During a California tour, the bandleader suffered a nervous breakdown, leaving Davis stranded far from his musical home in New York. Both artists eventually made it back to the city, and Miles rejoined Parker. He soon quit, though, over disagreements about personnel and money issues.

NEW DIRECTIONS

Around the time that Davis was ending his stint in Charlie Parker's band, he got to know arranger Gil Evans. Evans' New York apartment had become a meeting place for young musicians who were dissatisfied with the direction of jazz. The group included pianist John Lewis and saxophonist Gerry Mulligan.

Miles became a member of this informal club. The association resulted in an ensemble of musicians that performed as the Miles Davis Nonet. While the group was not particularly well received in New York club performances, it did make a number

Miles Davis

of landmark recordings. In 1957, they were released together as the album *Birth of the Cool.*

Chapter 9 introduced us to the *Birth of the Cool*, which marked a new direction for jazz. The compositions broke from the high-octane sound of bebop to create a new style. The laidback arrangements fit perfectly with Miles' own approach to playing the

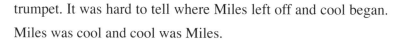

trumpet. It was hard to tell where Miles left off and cool began. Miles was cool and cool was Miles.

Others would develop the new cool sound more fully than Davis, who went on to other things musically. It would become a repeating pattern in his life. Miles would serve as pioneer and leading light for a movement then he would move on. This was both inspirational and frustrating for jazz fans to witness.

It is difficult to fully understand Davis' need to stake an artistic claim and then leave it behind. Maybe it was fueled by a need for constant innovation. Maybe it was a type of restlessness. One of the musicians who played with him once asked Davis why he didn't perform ballads more often. Miles answered, "Because I love playing them too much."

MILES IN THE 1950S

The early 1950s brought difficulties for Davis. In particular, he developed the same dependence on drugs that plagued other jazz musicians of the era. His addiction would last for several years and hinder his career. At the same time, he experienced depression and felt unappreciated by jazz critics.

Davis began to earn a reputation of being difficult to work with during this time. He could be withdrawn yet quick to become angry. At one point in his career, Miles even turned his back to audiences when performing. It was of course seen as an insult, and he was heckled for it.

Despite it all, Davis remained productive during the first half of the 1950s. 1954 saw the release of *Walkin'* for the young Prestige label. The album featured a small ensemble with Davis as its leader. The title track marked yet another new musical direction; its bluesy, churchy groove was one of the first recordings in the style that would come to be known as hard bop.

A year later, Davis formed a new quintet. It featured the hard bop pianist Red Garland and the virtuosic young bassist Paul Chambers. It also included drummer Philly Joe Jones and a largely unknown talent on tenor saxophone, John Coltrane. The group would make a number of influential recordings over the next couple of years.

The Miles Davis Quintet played a variety of styles within the jazz idiom. The group helped Davis continue to pursue hard bop. It also played bebop and standards from the Great American Songbook. Musical breadth became one of its legacies.

In 1957, Columbia Records released the quintet's *'Round About Midnight* album. It featured a stellar interpretation of the Thelonious Monk ballad "'Round Midnight." Davis plays his trumpet with a Harmon mute, his ringing notes hanging like a smoky haze in the air. Live performance of the same piece at the 1955 Newport Jazz Festival brought Davis the critical acclaim he felt he had been denied up to that point.

The quintet disbanded for a while but then reformed as a sextet with the addition of Cannonball Adderley on alto saxophone. The expanded group recorded the album *Milestones* in 1958.

MODAL MILES

It had been less than 10 years since the *Birth of the Cool* sessions. Davis had already gone beyond it to help father hard bop. With *Milestones,* he was instrumental in the birth of yet another style, modal jazz.

A mode is a collection of pitches with one of them serving as the tonic—the center or home pitch. Only two modes are common in most European and American music, major and minor.

Using only the white keys of a piano, the major mode has C as its tonic. Make A the tonic and we have the minor mode.

Modes possess particular qualities. For example, the minor mode tends to sound sad to our ears. Other modes beyond major and minor are possible, each having a distinct quality. Modal jazz uses these uncommon modes to explore these qualities and their musical potential.

Like cool jazz and hard bop, modal jazz was partly a reaction to bebop. The harmonic progressions of bebop had become increasingly complex. A jazz musician almost needed an advanced degree in music theory to handle the chord changes of a song while improvising.

Modal jazz helped put the musical emphasis back on rhythmic groove. Instead of being clogged with complex harmonies, a modal piece relied on a single mode for musicians to use as inspiration. It changed the nature of improvisation. Instead of negotiating complicated chords, a player was free to explore the implications of a single mode. As with cool jazz, less was more.

Milestones gave the world a small taste of modal jazz. Davis' next album, *Kind of Blue* (1959), served up a modal feast. The album remains one of

LIVES AND TIMES

Rosa Parks One day in December 1955, secretary Rosa Parks refused to give up her seat on a Montgomery, Alabama city bus so that a white person could sit down. At that time, black bus passengers were expected to sit in the back of buses in many cities. Parks' simple but courageous act inspired others and made her a symbol of the American civil-rights movement.

I Have a Dream In August 1963, civil-rights activist Dr. Martin Luther King, Jr. led the March on Washington for Jobs and Freedom. The climax of the event came when King gave an address from the steps of the Lincoln Memorial passionately calling for racial equality and harmony. Known as the "I Have a Dream" speech, it stands one of the most stirring addresses in American political history.

Moon Landing The Soviet Union's 1957 launch of Sputnik, the first human-made object to orbit the Earth, sparked a fierce space race between that country and the United States. The ultimate goal became to land a person on the moon. That was accomplished in 1969 when American astronaut Neil Armstrong stepped foot on the lunar surface as part of NASA's Apollo program.

Beatlemania When the Beatles first landed in New York, in 1964, it set off fan hysteria across America. The fervor for the mop-top rock quartet from England was so intense that the term Beatlemania was coined to describe it. Soon after their arrival from London, they appeared on the Ed Sullivan variety television show. Over 70 million Americans tuned in, a record for the time.

the most popular in the history of jazz. It included a number of modal works that have become jazz standards—"So What," "All Blues," and "Blue in Green."

SO WHAT

The *Kind of Blue* recording of "So What" shows what modal blues is all about. It begins with piano and bass exploring the piece's Dorian mode without a beat. It is 30 seconds into the performance before a pulse appears. This happens when Paul Chambers starts playing the melody.

"So What" is one of only a few jazz compositions in which the string bass alone carries the melody. Trumpet and saxophones answer each of its lines with a harmonized two-note statement. The middle section of the melody stays the same. It is just a half step higher.

SUGGESTED LISTENING

MILES DAVIS
"E.S.P."
"Jeru"
"'Round Midnight"
"Summertime"
"Walkin'"

JOHN COLTRANE
"Afro Blue"
"Giant Steps"
"My Favorite Things"

Modal jazz places much emphasis on harmonic color. In "So What," the pianist, Bill Evans, shades the performance with pitches farther apart than in a standard chord. The voicing is so distinctive it has been dubbed the "So What" chord.

Davis solos first. His relaxed playing allows him to discover the potential of the Dorian mode. He moves about, emphasizing different notes as he plays. Some create a musical tension with the rhythm section. Others release the tension. Miles toys with this type of tension and release throughout his solo.

Coltrane takes the next solo on tenor saxophone. Like Davis, he uses a straight tone with no vibrato. This creates a cool sound. However, there is also a bright edge to Coltrane's tone that is anything but cool. His solo is also busier than Davis'.

Adderley follows Coltrane. His solo has more of a bebop feel to it. It is busier even than Coltrane's solo. Adderley displays a relaxed agility as he plays run after run up and down his instrument.

Bill Evans solos on piano last. He plays a few single-note phrases. Most of the solo consists of tight chord *clusters* (closely spaced pitches), though. The notes he chooses give the clusters a noticeable bite. Evans then melts into the background riff for the song. The horns join him a few measures later, and the band closes out the song with a return to the head.

FROM MODAL TO FUSION

Miles Davis continued in the same musical vein for a number of years. He fronted small ensembles featuring up-and-coming jazz musicians and played a mix of modal jazz and hard bop. He also served up something different now and then. 1958 brought *Porgy and Bess*, an album of songs from the George Gershwin opera of the same name. Longtime Davis collaborator Gil Evans arranged the music for the album, as well as for Miles' *Sketches of Spain* (1960), an album that included the music of Spanish classical composers Joaquín Rodrigo and Manuel de Falla.

During the 1960s, Miles music began hinting at something different. Some of his recordings included electric instruments, and new grooves began popping up. Davis was coming under the influence of rock 'n' roll and funk. He was finding inspiration in the music of such artists as James Brown, Sly Stone, and Jimi Hendrix.

With the 1969 album *In a Silent Way*, Miles quit hinting. He gave birth to an all-out fusion of jazz and rock, surrounding

himself with young musicians who enjoyed playing electric instruments. Miles also began miking his trumpet and running the
output through a wah-wah, an effects pedal normally used by
guitarists.

On 1970's *Bitches Brew*, Davis continued exploring jazz-rock
fusion. This double album enjoyed much commercial success. It
also led to fierce accusations that Davis was a traitor to jazz. The
recording featured electric instruments and rock grooves rather
than traditional instruments and swing rhythms. About the only
thing that seemed to remain of jazz was an emphasis on improvisation. (Miles' role in the fusion movement will be further discussed in the next chapter.)

The following years would bring a shift from fusion to funk.
Davis withdrew professionally during the last half of the 1970s.
He apparently needed a rest and again suffered from addiction.
When he reemerged in the 1980s, he continued to explore rock.
Doo-Bop (1992) was Miles' final album. Released after his death,
its exploration of hip-hop shows him to be a fierce innovator to
the end.

Catching the 'Trane

*I've found you've got to look back at the
old things and see them in a new light.*
—JOHN COLTRANE

Quite a few jazz greats have come from North Carolina. Thelonious Monk was born in Rocky Mount, and Dizzy Gillespie
went to high school in the little town of Laurinburg. Saxophonist
John Coltrane came from Hamlet, a town not far from Laurinburg. He then lived in High Point. As a teenager, Coltrane moved

to Philadelphia and became a sailor in 1945.

The same year he joined the Navy, Coltrane saw Charlie Parker perform live. The bebop great had as much of an impact on Coltrane as he had on a young Miles Davis. He later remem-

John and Alice Coltrane

bered, "The first time I heard Bird play, it hit me right between the eyes."

As a young musician, Coltrane performed occasionally with Parker and Dizzy Gillespie. A big break came for Coltrane in

1955. That year, Miles Davis asked him to join a new quintet. (We discussed the importance of the Miles Davis Quintet above and briefly considered Coltrane's solo on "So What.")

During his years with Davis, Coltrane periodically stepped out on his own. Notably, he played with Thelonious Monk and released a hard bop recording under his own name. *Blue Trane* (1957) featured an ensemble of leading young musicians and four tracks composed by Coltrane. The group included Coltrane's band mates from the Miles Davis Quintet, bassist Paul Chambers and drummer Philly Joe Jones. It also proclaimed the nickname he had come to be known by, Trane.

GIANT STEPS

Coltrane released a monumental recording of original works, *Giant Steps*, at the end of his time in Davis's band. The best-known composition from this 1960 album is the title track. The complexities of the rapid chord progression used in "Giant Steps" still make a musician's jaw drop.

Trane's improvisation on "Giant Steps" also fills a listener with wonder. It has become one of the most famous solos in jazz history. It features fast, dense runs of notes. These are heard in many Coltrane improvisations and have been dubbed "sheets of sound."

The "Giant Steps" recording begins with Coltrane playing the melody right away. The tempo is extremely fast. Tommy Flanagan shadows Trane on piano, playing tight block chords in rhythm with him. Art Taylor plays a quick swinging rhythm on ride cymbal. The melody is brief and only contains one section but goes through three keys.

Coltrane immediately launches into his improvisation by laying down sheets of sound. His solo lasts for many choruses and never pauses. It is an astonishing perpetual motion of phrases that simply fly by like fence posts past a speeding car. A person has to listen to it many times slowed down to fully grasp all of the ideas it contains.

Flanagan's solo is shorter and more halting. Who can blame him? No mere mortal could compete with Trane's musical on-slaught. He soon gives the helm back to the band-leader. Coltrane reenters and improvises a little more, as if to say, "It's OK. I've got it." The band then returns to the head to play out the piece.

For many musicians, particularly saxophon-ists, Coltrane's playing stands as the greatest achievement in jazz improvisation. To this day, they devoutly study his approach. In particular, being able to improvise well on "Giant Steps" at full tempo is considered to be a mark of arrival as a true jazz musician.

TRANEING IN ON NEW TERRITORY

Like Miles Davis, Coltrane tended to forsake the musical direc-tions he helped pioneer in favor of pursuing new territory. In the years immediately after *Giant Steps*, Trane turned more to modal jazz. He also started incorporating ideas from beyond jazz, in-cluding the Indian *raga* system of modal and melodic organiza-tion.

Coltrane also began exploring free jazz. Fellow saxophonists like Eric Dolphy and Ornette Coleman joined him in doing so. The movement tried to tear down what were seen as the stifling conventions of beat, chord progression, and fixed structure. Free jazz performances and recordings became formless improvisatory interactions among the performers. The Coltrane album *As-cension* (1966) stands as a landmark example of the approach.

This pursuit of free jazz perplexed many critics. They began to see Coltrane, whom they had previously held up as a leading light of modern jazz, as a traitor. Free jazz also became known

John Coltrane

as anti-jazz, and many of its creators did not disagree. They felt even the term jazz had become confining.

During the same period in the 1960s, Coltrane headed up a

renowned quartet that combined hard bop with free ideas. The band included Elvin Jones on drums, McCoy Tyner on piano, and Jimmy Garrison on bass. The group's recordings found Trane to be on a profound spiritual quest, with a particular interest in Eastern religions.

Like a number of other jazz greats, John Coltrane did not enjoy a long life. He died at the age of 40. Early years of addiction took their toll on him. Some also blame his all-consuming drive to achieve unattainable goals as a musician, leading to overwork and a disregard for his own physical needs.

The Legacy of Miles and Coltrane

Both Miles Davis and John Coltrane showed the world that jazz could be music of profound artistic expression. Listen to their performances and you hear musical perfection few others have achieved. They certainly deserve inclusion on a Mount Rushmore of jazz.

More than that, the work of Davis and Coltrane stands among the highest musical expressions—right next to Louis Armstrong and Charlie Parker, and also alongside Bach and Beethoven, Robert Johnson, and Jimi Hendrix.

There is more to the legacy of John Coltrane. He made the pursuit of jazz a profound spiritual quest. In recognition of this, the African Orthodox Church considers him to be a saint. Their services even feature his music.

Jaco Pastorius

FUSION

Fusion is the joining together of two or more things to create a new entity. There have been a number of examples in the history of jazz. The first took place when ragtime melded with blues as played by the brass bands of New Orleans. The result was traditional jazz.

Another form of musical fusion happened in the 1940s. Jazz fused with Cuban rhythms to create Latin jazz. A decade later, jazz bounded with R&B and gospel to produce hard bop. Then, jazz combined with Brazilian rhythms to create bossa nova in the 1950s.

When people talk about jazz fusion though, most often simply called fusion, they are usually referring to another blending. Towards the end of the 1960s, a few jazz musicians began experimenting. They mixed jazz with rock 'n' roll. As you know, Miles Davis served as an important pioneer of this new music.

Fusion hit its full stride in the 1970s. Groups like Weather Report and the Mahavishnu Orchestra stretched the definition of jazz as they created enthusiastic new audiences. As we'll see, fusion remains popular to this day.

Electric Miles

I'll play it first and tell you what it is later.
—MILES DAVIS

Miles Davis was already a jazz legend by the late 1960s. He had cut his teeth playing bebop with Charlie Parker. He had then helped father cool jazz in the late 1940s as well as hard bop and modal jazz in the 1950s. He had also served as the leader of a stellar quintet that featured such jazz greats as John Coltrane and Cannonball Adderley.

Davis formed a new quintet in the mid-1960s with younger musicians. The group consisted of Wayne Shorter on saxophone, Herbie Hancock on piano, Ron Carter on bass, and Tony Williams on drums. Together, they recorded a series of influential albums that revealed an open, loosely organized approach. It came to be known as free bop. These musicians would go on to become important figures in their own right.

Something else was different. On a couple of the albums, electric instruments appeared. Specifically, the Fender Rhodes keyboard replaced the piano and electric bass took the place of acoustic. It was a suggestion of things to come.

During this time, Davis became interested in acid rock and funk music. Supposedly, a concert by Sly and the Family Stone made a big impression on him. On seeing the audience response, Davis realized the power such music held. He came away convinced that jazz needed to adapt.

IN A SILENT WAY

The 1969 album *In a Silent Way* clearly shows the affect of rock music on Davis. Historians generally recognize it as the first fusion album. It contains only two tracks, each clocking in at over 18 minutes and lasting the entire side of an LP record. Electric keyboard and bass entirely replace their acoustic counterparts, and the ensemble now even includes electric guitar, courtesy of John McLaughlin.

It is not quite right to say that *In a Silent Way* blends jazz with rock. The music is clearly not straight-ahead jazz but it does not sound like rock either. What *In a Silent Way* takes from rock is its approach.

NOT JAZZ AND NOT ROCK

During the 1960s, acid rock groups like the Grateful Dead and Pink Floyd engaged in grand experimentation. They performed long, freeform improvisations that often had no clear melody, harmony, or even rhythm. This is what seems to have most inspired the musical approach heard on *In a Silent Way*.

In important ways, acid rock is similar to free jazz. Both share the same free-flowing approach that emphasizes group improvisation over musical conventions. While Davis was not a free jazz musician, the free bop he played was influenced by it. So, we can also see *In a Silent Way* as being an electrification of free jazz.

Rolling Stone magazine described the album this way, "It is not rock and roll, but it's nothing stereotyped as jazz either. All at once, it owes almost as much to the techniques developed by rock improvisers in the last four years as to Davis' jazz background."

The article continues, "It is part of a transcendental new music which flushes categories away and, while using musical devices from all styles and cultures, is defined mainly by its deep emotion and unaffected originality."

Jazz critics and fans were not as enthusiastic about *In a Silent Way*. Many actually saw it as a musical betrayal. Davis' stature as a jazz musician made the matter worse. It was if Beethoven had turned his back on classical music, even slapped it in the face.

MILES' CONTROVERSIAL *BREW*

The next year brought further insult to jazz purists. The double album *Bitches Brew* solidified Davis' exploration of freeform improvisation and the use of electric instruments. It also includes a track with an obvious connection to music beyond jazz.

In terms of groove, "Miles Davis Runs the Voodoo Down" is pure funk. It is also the least free-wheeling track on the album. For this combination of reasons, it proved influential for fusion. It showed that a jazz approach to performance could be applied to music with a different beat.

Miles continued to explore fusion in his next albums. The influence of funk became stronger, and he began playing his trumpet through a wah-wah pedal. To reach a larger audience, he opened for touring rock acts. Nothing matched the success or influence of *Bitches Brew* on the development of fusion, though.

Weather Report

Whatever you want to call it all, it is all improvised music. —JOE ZAWINUL

The fusion of jazz with rock and funk music took full shape in the 1970s. Veterans of Miles Davis' electrified ensembles struck out to form their own bands. As they did, they developed the musical ideas Davis had pioneered into a distinct style all their own.

Weather Report reigned as one of the top bands of the fu-

Weather Report

sion movement throughout the decade. The group was founded in 1970 by saxophonist Wayne Shorter, a Miles Davis alumnus, and keyboardist Joe Zawinul. Czech-born bass player Miroslav Vitous, drummer Alphonse Mouzon, and Brazilian percussionist Airto Moreira rounded out the original lineup.

The band's self-titled 1971 debut album was largely acoustic and seemed to look back to the free improvisation heard in Davis' music. It was more experimental than fusion. The influential jazz magazine *Downbeat* called it "music beyond category" and named it as their album of the year.

The next albums released by Weather Report started to make a transition. They moved towards electric instruments, especially the synthesizer, and more structured, funk-oriented tracks. This change was causing a rift in the band and led to Vitous leaving the group.

With a new bass player and drummer, Weather Report recorded its breakout album, *Mysterious Traveller* (1974). It debuted the band's full-blown fusion sound. There was strong emphasis on Zawinul playing synthesizers, clear-cut compositions, and funk- and rock-inspired grooves. The record again won Album of the Year from *Downbeat*.

JACO PASTORIUS

A brash young bass player supposedly approached Zawinul one night after a concert. He told the Weather Report keyboardist he had been disappointed with the performance. He also introduced himself as the world's greatest bass player. Actually, the young man had reason to brag. He was in fact a phenomenal performer.

John "Jaco" Francis Anthony Pastorius III (1951–1987) was then still in his mid-20s. Yet, he had already developed a revolutionary approach to the electric bass. A true virtuoso, he could play lighting fast runs and make his instrument seem to sing in its upper register. He also excelled at playing harmonics, high notes created by touching the strings lightly at certain points.

Although he initially scoffed at Pastorius, Zawinul got to know the young bass player. Soon enough he recognized Pastorius' talent and asked him to join Weather Report. With his addition, the band would go on to its greatest artistic achievements.

BIRDLAND

The 1977 album *Heavy Weather* features Weather Report's most recognizable work. "Birdland" proved unusually popular for a jazz composition. It takes its title from the famed New York jazz club whose name memorializes the nickname of bebop legend Charlie Parker. Other artists, like big band leader Maynard Ferguson and the vocal group Manhattan Transfer, began recording the tune, and it became a standard.

In large part, the popularity of "Birdland" comes from its catchy melody and clear structure. It was a far cry from the formless improvisations of the earliest fusion music. The style had developed away from the avant-garde and closer to the musical mainstream.

"Birdland" begins with Joe Zawinul playing a low, syncopated keyboard line. He is on synthesizer and each note has an electronic "bwow" tone. The rest of the band minus Wayne Shorter then enters. The drums and tambourine lay down a tight rhythm. Jaco Pastorius plays the first part of the melody extremely high on the electric bass; Zawinul shadows him on acoustic piano.

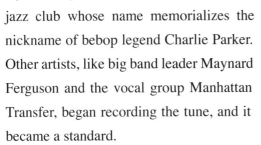

LIVES AND TIMES

Rock Revolution A great shift in popular music took place in the 1950s. During the earlier part of the 20th century, jazz dominated popular music. A new beat inspired young Americans after Word War II. As it did, rock 'n' roll began to displace jazz on radio stations and record store shelves.

Generation Gap The baby boomers born in postwar America began to question many of their parents' values. They came to doubt what they had been taught about lifestyle, religion, education, drugs, and a range of other issues. A counter-culture developed in opposition to established social norms. It eventually faded away as boomers grew to full adulthood.

Vietnam War Opposition to America's military involvement in Vietnam helped define the baby boomer generation. It led to a large-scale peace movement and demonstrations on college campuses across the country. In opposition to the war, many young men refused to serve in the military.

Throughout its history, jazz has depended on the AABA melodic form found in Tin Pan Alley songs. The main melody in this scheme is found in the A sections. B serves as a bridge to and from A. "Birdland" relies more on the modern form found in most rock songs. Here, A serves as a verse that leads into B — the chorus that carries the main melody of the song.

The reliance of "Birdland" on modern song form shows an even greater fusion with rock music. It helped make "Birdland" more approachable and radio-friendly. The vocal group Manhattan Transfer in fact scored a pop hit with their recording of it using lyrics written by Jon Hendricks, an originator of *vocalese* (jazz singing in which lyrics are written for what was originally instrumental).

Shorter enters on saxophone to carry the melody during the chorus of the Weather Report recording. Other instruments shadow him. Pastorius plays a line that is more countermelody than a regular bass part.

"Birdland" does not follow modern song form to the letter. Instead, Zawinul plays a new repetitive melody on piano after the chorus. Drums and tambourine continue ticking away underneath. Shorter interrupts the vamp with an assertive but lyrical line that seems to sing the title.

Next comes a short breakdown section in which the keyboard and bass play off of one another. A refrain follows. Shorter takes the lead on this as layer upon layer joins in. The melody for the refrain is so infectious that it begs for the listener to hum along.

After the refrain comes a second, synthesizer-driven breakdown. Various parts are added to create a wonderful polyphonic stew of sound. Shorter then plays an improvised solo on tenor saxophone. The band plays a descending line behind him. Everyone eventually melts out of this section.

The rest of the "Birdland" recording serves up a repeat of its various melodies. It ends with a return to the hum-along refrain. It repeats for over a minute and a half and seems like an anthem to the jazz club that inspired the composition's title. Meanwhile, on synth, Zawinul improvises merrily away above the melody.

Other Fusion Groups

Jazz has borrowed from other genres of music and also has lent itself to other genres of music. —HERBIE HANCOCK

The fusion bands founded by other Miles Davis alumni also enjoyed success during the 1970s. One was Return to Forever, headed up by keyboardist Chick Corea. His musical path was somewhat different from that of Shorter and Weather Report. The early years for Return to Forever emphasized Latin grooves inspired by the band's Brazilian members, vocalist Flora Purim

Return to Forever

and percussionist Airto Moreira.

From 1973, Return to Forever's sound became more influenced by rock. Over time, synthesizer, electric bass, and distorted electric guitar, as well as rock and funk grooves made their way into the band's sound. The Latin influences melted away.

The band's 1976 album *Romantic Warrior* stands as its greatest achievement. A trio of top-notch musicians joins Corea. Stanley Clarke plays electric bass, Lenny White is on drums, and Al Di Meola can be heard on both electric and acoustic guitar. Together, they play fast, tight melodic lines. In this and other ways, *Romantic Warrior* seems to reflect the progressive rock of its time.

HERBIE HANCOCK

Keyboardist Herbie Hancock was associated with Miles Davis through most of the 1960s. During that time he also started to strike out on his own as a leader. His 1965 album *Maiden Voyage* is an important example of modal jazz. It contained several compositions that have become jazz standards, including the title track.

In 1973 Hancock assembled saxophonist Bennie Maupin, drummer Harvey Mason, and others to record an album of funk-inspired music. *Head Hunters* represents a defining moment in the history of fusion. Although it was criticized as being overly commercial, it brought the music to a wide audience.

Funk has always been about groove above all else. In a track like "Funky Women" by James Brown or "Atomic Dog" by George Clinton, the melody and lyrics are almost irrelevant. Likewise, there is really no chord progression. A song often becomes more of an extended jam, especially in live performance.

"Chameleon" from *Head Hunters* clocks in at over 15 minutes and captures the essence of funk perfectly. It begins with Hancock playing a syncopated bass line on synthesizer. Other layers join one by one. Drums lay down a funky groove, guitar plays scratch rhythms, and the clavinet adds a staccato, syncopated line.

In the true spirit of funk, this groove is allowed to simmer like soup stock for over a minute and a half. When the melody does enter, it is simple, repetitive, communal, and rides atop the continuing groove. This is also funk.

What ultimately makes "Chameleon" fusion rather than out-

Herbie Hancock

and-out funk is what happens during the rest of the recording. Unlike the music of Brown or Clinton, the emphasis is clearly placed on extended improvisations. The members of the band solo one after the other, exploring the groove.

The tag heard at the melody returns at the end of solos. It is taken through some interesting harmonic manipulations. This too marks "Chameleon" as fusion. Hancock's long Fender Rhodes keyboard solo in the middle of the recording in fact becomes quite jazzy. The recording ends with a return to the original groove and Maupin soloing away into a fade.

A SIX-STRING THING

Fusion became a vehicle for a number of fine guitarists. They include John McLaughlin (b. 1942), who also recorded with Miles Davis in the late 1960s. An astounding virtuoso, he founded the Mahavishnu Orchestra with drummer Billy Cobham (a fellow Davis alumnus) and Czech keyboardist Jan Hammer. From the

John McLaughlin

beginning, the ensemble also included a violinist, the original one being Jerry Goodman.

Like jazz great John Coltrane before him, McLaughlin found inspiration in the spiritual teachings of India. His guru in fact bestowed upon McLaughlin the name Mahavishnu. It means "divine compassion, power and justice." He used the name for his band as well.

We have already seen several different approaches to fusion. The original Mahavishnu Orchestra, for its part, seemed to channel the spirit of rock guitarist Jimi Hendrix. The music was virtuosic and powerful. It burned with molten runs played on distorted guitar over complex time signatures.

During the latter half of the 1970s, McLaughlin turned away from the electrified sound of the Mahavishnu Orchestra. He went on to found the acoustic ensemble Shakti with Indian violinist L. Shankar. It became a pioneering group in the world music fusion realm.

PAT METHENY

Pat Metheny (b. 1954) is another guitarist who found much success with fusion. He is part of a younger generation that studied jazz in college rather than in apprenticeships with veteran musicians. After leaving school, he soon formed the Pat Metheny Group. The band's second album, 1980's *American Garage*, enjoyed unusual success for a jazz release. In particular, its lead track, "(Cross the) Heartland" crossed over to other musical markets.

With such compositions, Metheny helped establish a new subgenre of jazz. A spin-off of fusion, smooth jazz emphasizes poppy arrangements, gentle tempos, and even more complete fusing with popular music. It also features the signature sounds of soloists like saxophonist Kenny G, guitarist Earl Klugh, and pianist Dave Grusin.

Smooth jazz has developed into a staple of light radio. Some

Pat Metheny

stations are actually entirely dedicated to it. While a number of serious jazz artists have plied the waters of smooth jazz, it has still gained the reputation of being artistically questionable. The online *Urban Dictionary* even dismisses it as "fuzak"—music "so innocuous as to round the bend and be remarkably obnoxious."

Perhaps that's one reason why Metheny has varied his work to include projects of a more experimental nature, such as his collaboration with free jazz saxophonist Ornette Coleman on the album *Song X*, as well as more straightahead jazz projects. His recent *Orchestrion Project* combines man and machines in a unique live performance.

JAZZY ROCK

Fusion has actually been a two-way street. Jazz musicians have been inspired by rock and funk. At the same time, rock and funk musicians have been inspired by jazz. For example, you can certainly hear it in the music of an artist like Stevie Wonder, on his song "Sir Duke" and in Wonder's harmonic approach in general. Several influential jazz-rock bands also began recording from the late 1960s on.

Chicago combined a rock band with the type of wind instruments long associated with jazz—trumpet, trombone, and saxophone. The group became known for songs like "Make Me Smile" and "25 or 6 to 4." They married rock with in-your-face horn arrangements that displayed clear jazz overtones. Over the years, the musical style of Chicago has become much more middle-of-the-road.

Blood, Sweat & Tears was another jazz-rock band from the same period. It was created by some of the finest New York studio musicians at the time. While Chicago tended to be one part jazz and two parts rock, Blood, Sweat and Tears inverted the recipe. Songs like "Spinning Wheel" and "You've Made Me So Very Happy" contain obvious jazz elements, especially in their solo sections. The band even had a hit with a cover of Billie Holiday's "God Bless the Child."

British rock guitarist Jeff Beck released two classic jazz-influenced albums in the 1970s: *Blow by Blow* and *Wired*.

Jazz inspired some other pop groups active in the 1970s, notably Steely Dan. The fusion movement also inspired funk. One of the greatest funk bands of all time, Tower of Power, clearly bears its mark. In the horn arrangements of songs like "What Is Hip?" and "Get Your Feet Back on the Ground," we hear a tight fusing of funk with jazz ideas. The improvisation of members like saxophonist Lenny Pickett also brought jazz-like soloing to funk.

The Legacy of Fusion

The baby boomers who came of age in the 1960s and '70s had new musical tastes. While their parents were raised on big band swing, the boomers grew up on the Beatles, Jimi Hendrix, the Grateful Dead, and James Brown. Jazz was simply not baby boomer music. Rock and funk were and they held great power. Miles Davis recognized this. The fusion movement brought some of the power of rock and funk to jazz.

It is said, "If you can't beat 'em, join 'em." By the late 1960s, jazz was suffering commercially at the hands of the rock revolution. Fusion allowed jazz musicians to reach out to baby boomers and find a new audience. As it did, groups like Weather Report and the Mahavishnu Orchestra could play the same concert halls and arenas as rock acts.

Although synthesizers and guitars emerged as a force during the fusion era, wind players also started experimenting with electronic sounds. Saxophonist Michael Brecker used a special wind controller to play synthesized sounds. Others began using echo and other effects to create new sounds.

A number of the artists who pioneered early fusion eventually retreated from it. They turned off their synthesizers and amplifiers and returned to acoustic instruments. They did so to begin a new exploration of jazz in and of itself, leading to the jazz revival we will read about in our next chapter. Miles Davis, though, kept exlporing new ground with fusion.

The retreat from fusion by its pioneers is understandable.

They were not baby boomers, and so rock was not their natural form of musical expression. Younger musicians, like Pat Metheny, would be more the ones to carry fusion through the 1980s

Mindi Abair

and beyond. Today, artists like Brian Culbertson, Candy Dulfer, and Mindi Abair show the influence of the fusion generation.

There is no longer an official fusion movement. Still, fusion continues to this day, in part through the sounds of smooth jazz. Artists of more serious intent will occasionally undertake fusion projects, and pioneers of the style will also sometimes embark on reunion tours that help keep alive the spirit of the music.

Wynton Marsalis

THE JAZZ REVIVAL

By 1980, the fusion movement had swept away all other forms of jazz. Or so it seemed. Bands like Weather Report and Return to Forever had created a new world. Electric guitar and synthesizer had taken the place of the saxophone and acoustic piano. Miles Davis was still playing trumpet, but electrified through a wah-wah pedal.

More than that, rock and funk rhythms had all but replaced the swinging eighth notes that had always been a hallmark of jazz. From the traditional jazz of New Orleans through the modal forms of John Coltrane, a swinging pulse had been the rhythmic underpinning of jazz. With fusion, it was all but gone.

But swing-based jazz was like a boxer who had been knocked down but not out. Soon it got up off the canvas and started swinging once more. As it did, earlier styles came together. Musicians started thinking of them as part of a single whole they began to refer to as straight-ahead jazz. Momentum built and within a few years, a full-blown revival of straight-ahead jazz was underway.

Back to the Future

I dress up a certain way because I respect the music. —WYNTON MARSALIS

New Orleans gave birth to jazz in the early decades of the 20th century. The traditional jazz born there went on to conquer Chicago, New York, and the rest of the country during the 1920s. It experienced a decline in popularity with the coming of swing in the next decade.

There were attempts to revive traditional jazz in the years that followed. The 1950s saw an especially big push. Older artists enjoyed a new status as esteemed elders, and young artists emerged, including trumpeter Al Hirt and clarinetist Pete Fountain.

The 1970s brought with it renewed interest in ragtime. In particular, Scott Joplin became popular again. His music received a big boost when it was used in the hit movie *The Sting* (1973). As ragtime enjoyed a revival, interest also increased for traditional jazz.

The Preservation Hall Jazz Band has played a key role in carrying forward the New Orleans legacy. Back home, the group serves as the house band at the Preservation Hall in the city's French Quarter. It has also toured extensively since the 1960s, bringing authentic sounds to fans around the world.

A new breed of New Orleans bands emerged in the city during the 1970s into the 1980s. Groups like the Dirty Dozen Brass Band and Rebirth Brass Band began mixing old-school strains with funk, bebop, and other styles. While less traditional than the

Preservation Hall Jazz Band, they helped keep the spirit of New Orleans music alive.

Dirty Dozen Brass Band

A number of the musicians who helped define this new brass band sound got their start in the same way. As children, they played in the Fairview Baptist Church Marching Band led by Danny Barker. One of them would go on to become a principle player in the jazz revival movement.

WYNTON MARSALIS

The son of New Orleans jazz pianist Ellis Marsalis, Wynton Marsalis (b. 1961) joined the Fairview Church band at age eight. Like Miles Davis, he moved to New York to study at Juilliard upon graduation from high school. Also like Davis, he soon found himself playing professionally. He started in Art Blakey's Jazz Messengers and quickly went on to perform with an array of other jazz greats.

Marsalis emerged as a leading light of the straight-ahead jazz revival during the 1980s. One of his most important roles was in helping to create Jazz at Lincoln Center. It has grown into an important sponsor of jazz events, and Marsalis continues to serve as its director.

Marsalis has also become a frequent spokesperson for jazz. In interviews you will find him holding forth in profound terms about the great legacy of the music. He has helped assure that jazz receives the respect it deserves as a great art form.

WEARER OF MANY MUSICAL HATS

As a bandleader and trumpet player, Marsalis has spent a great deal of energy documenting in sound the jazz of earlier eras. He has even taken us back to New Orleans' Congo Square to hear the roots of jazz. Much of this work has been with the Jazz at Lincoln Center Orchestra.

There is another side to Marsalis. He is a trained classical musician who has performed as a soloist with leading orchestras around the world. He has even composed original orchestral music that blends classical styles with jazz.

Marsalis has not been without a few critics. Some of the strongest have been other leading jazz artists, including Miles Davis. They have questioned Marsalis' musicianship. Some critics also feel he has championed only a certain part of jazz's heritage. Others believe that his efforts to dignify jazz have had a stifling effect, turning it into a stilted museum piece.

BRANFORD MARSALIS

Wynton Marsalis' older brother Branford has also played an important role in the revival of straight-ahead jazz. After studying at the Berklee College of Music in Boston, he began performing with such jazz greats as Art Blakey and Dizzy Gillespie. He is best known for heading up his own quartet.

The bulk of Branford Marsalis' music has been straight-ahead jazz. However, he has parted from that path quite a bit. In 1980, he toured and recorded with the rock star Sting. Then, in the early 1990s, he served as the bandleader for television's *Tonight Show*. After that, he organized Buckshot LeFonque—a project that blended jazz with classical, R&B, and hip-hop.

IT'S ALL ABOUT SWING

What are the musical elements that make up straight-ahead jazz as performed by the Marsalis brothers and others? The most important is a swinging rhythm with four beats per measure. In earlier chapters, we learned that this was not a trait found in the traditional jazz of New Orleans. There, two beat measures and a stiffer subdivision of the beat served as the rhythmic foundation.

SUGGESTED LISTENING

WYNTON MARSALIS
"Cherokee"
"Root Groove"
"Soon All Will Know"

JOSHUA REDMAN
"East of the Sun (West of the Sun)"
"Salt Peanuts"
"Wish"

CASSANDRA WILSON
"Find Him"
"The Very Thought of You"
"You Move Me"

More than anyone, Louis Armstrong taught jazz how to swing. In the late 1920s into the early 1930s, his playing displayed a rhythmic style that was more relaxed. He referred to it as swing. You can even hear Armstrong calling out to his pianist to "swing out there" in his 1931 recording of "Lazy River."

Armstrong's individual rhythmic style was so influential that swing became the basis for the next phase in the history of jazz. Even when the swing era died in the mid-1940s, bebop retained a swinging rhythm. It was subtler but present nonetheless. As jazz moved through the 1950s and into the 1960s, a swinging rhythm remained.

It was only the fusion of the 1970s that abandoned swing for other rhythms. More than anything, the jazz revival of the 1980s restored swing to the music.

Straight-ahead jazz relies on other aspects of its musical tradition. One is the type of walking bass lines that also developed in the 1930s. The piano also tends to comp chords in a rhythmic manner common since bebop. In addition, head arrangements of standards serve as the bread and butter of straight-ahead jazz.

Old Guard and a New Generation

Doesn't that fool know I recorded that song because I like it? —CECIL TAYLOR

The Marsalis brothers and others led a jazz revival in the 1980s. However, this does not mean that swing-oriented jazz disappeared completely in the 1970s. They may have been out of the spotlight, but some jazz musicians remained true to the legacy of Charlie Parker and John Coltrane.

Some of those who kept on keeping on were veteran artists who served as an unbroken bridge to jazz tradition. One of the most revered was pianist Oscar Peterson (1925–2007), who was discovered by the jazz impresario Norman Granz. Granz added Peterson to his 1949 Jazz at the Philharmonic show at Carnegie Hall. This catapulted Peterson to prominence, and he helped keep swinging jazz alive through the 1970s and beyond.

Phil Woods (b. 1931) was a proud keeper of the bebop flame during the 1970s. He got his start with the Birdland All Stars Tour and then Dizzy Gillespie in the 1950s. Interestingly, despite his devotion to bebop, Woods helped make the rock ballad "Just

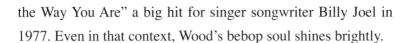

the Way You Are" a big hit for singer songwriter Billy Joel in 1977. Even in that context, Wood's bebop soul shines brightly.

YOUNGER ARTISTS

Some younger artists also gravitated toward swinging beats in the 1970s. They included fusion musicians who engaged in straight-ahead side projects. Even fusion stars like Herbie Hancock and Chick Corea did not turn their backs entirely on the swing element in jazz.

Terrence Blanchard

A childhood friend of Wynton Marsalis, New Orleans trumpeter Terence Blanchard (b. 1962) emerged as one of the young Turks of the jazz revival in the 1980s. He started his career in the band of legendary vibraphonist Lionel Hampton, who had played years before with Benny Goodman. Then, like Marsalis, Blanchard played with Art Blakey before striking out on his own.

In 1989, Blanchard recorded an album with fellow Blakey alumni Benny Green on piano and Javon Jackson on saxophone. *Prelude* shows the jazz revival already in full swing (pun intended). The group's recording of Duke Ellington's tribute to John

Coltrane, "Take the Coltrane," also shows how past and present could easily mix as part of the revival.

Ellington made the original recording of "Take the Coltrane" with Coltrane on an album they recorded together in 1962. Interestingly, Ellington's performance is quite bebop-like. Despite his famous remark that "bebop is like playing Scrabble with all the vowels removed," Ellington seems to channel the spirit of Thelonious Monk.

Coltrane's performance on this musical romp is much more novel. He seems to be channeling the spirit of no one but himself. The playing could only be his. The common ground for Ellington and Coltrane on of "Take the Coltrane" is the 12-bar blues form and the composition's swinging essence.

TAKE THE COLTRANE

Skip ahead more than 25 years and we find "Take the Coltrane" as recorded by Blanchard, Green, and Jackson. The tempo is slower and the feel a little cooler than the original. Green also adds a few stabbing notes in between the phrases of the melody that Ellington did not conceive.

After the head, Jackson takes the first improvised solo. His playing is bebop through and through, down to his double-time phrases. It swings hard. He even throws in a warped quote from the Ella Fitzgerald classic "A-Tisket, A-Tasket." It is fine playing, but Jackson is no Coltrane. No one is.

Blanchard follows with a trumpet solo. His solo is topnotch too, but it is interesting that this performance could be mistaken for one from Coltrane's time or even earlier. It is obviously looks to the past for inspiration. Actually, if anything, the playing is less adventurous than that on the original recording.

This reveals somewhat of a downside to the jazz revival. It is, by turns, conservative music. Jazz through much of its history was like the "boy a girl wouldn't want her mother to meet," according to a famous Duke Ellington observation. It was rebellious. It pushed limits. It explored new musical realms.

At times, the jazz revival actually seems to revere jazz tradition too much. Its musicians can sound like merely the current occupants of houses in a historic district. They can repaint their homes but only in their original colors, and they have agreed not to add new elements.

JAZZ GOES TO COLLEGE

Jazz education has blossomed at American colleges and universities since the 1970s. It actually got its start earlier at a few schools, particularly at the Berklee College of Music and North Texas State. However, in the 1970s, jazz in higher education went nationwide. It has done much to raise the overall level of performance among young musicians. Today's educated jazz musicians are usually well trained. They also understand the history and tradition of the music and their place within it. Some argue, though, that the institutionalization of jazz has also led to an over-standardization that goes against the fundamental spirit of the music.

LIVES AND TIMES

Yuppies By the 1980s, most baby boomers had abandoned counterculture ideas. They reengaged with mainstream values in the 1980s and many emerged as "young urban professionals," yuppies for short. As they did, they rediscovered more traditional aspects of American life, including jazz.

The Internet In the 1990s, America and the rest of the world started to go online. For jazz artists, it meant a way for them to connect with audiences more directly. For jazz fans, it meant almost instant access to the entire history of jazz as a recorded art form.

JOSHUA REDMAN

Saxophonist Joshua Redman (b. 1969) is one of the younger musicians who has embraced the tradition of jazz but still risen above it. From Redman's first albums in the early 1990s, critics held him up as something of a chosen figure. This was due in part to his heritage; he is the son of free jazz saxophonist Dewey Redman.

Although his family background made music a likely career path, Redman pursued a degree in social sciences at Harvard University. He graduated with honors and decided to take a one-

Joshua Redman

year break before going on to law school at Yale. For the year, he moved to New York and found himself jamming and gigging with top musicians in the city.

After winning the Thelonious Monk International Jazz Saxophone Competition, in 1991, Redman decided to give up on a law career and pursue music full time. For a while, he played as a sideman with jazz luminaries like saxophonist Joe Lovano, bassist Charlie Haden, and drummers Jack DeJohnette and Elvin Jones. Soon though, Redman was fronting his own band.

Following a self-titled debut, Redman released a number of well-received recordings during the 1990s. They emphasized

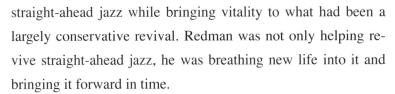

straight-ahead jazz while bringing vitality to what had been a largely conservative revival. Redman was not only helping revive straight-ahead jazz, he was breathing new life into it and bringing it forward in time.

Over the two decades of his career, Redman has not limited himself to straight-ahead jazz. He has continually grown as an artist and occasionally explored different musical avenues. He has even tried his hand at fusion. Still, he is most closely associated with the jazz revival.

INSOMNOMANIAC

From the 2009 record *Compass,* "Insomnomaniac" shows off Redman's ability to make jazz tradition sound new and fresh. The album as a whole takes much inspiration from the music of Sonny Rollins. In 1957, the tenor saxophone giant released two influential albums, *Way Out West* (1957) and *A Night at the Village Vanguard* (1957), with a trio instead of a quartet. It did away with the piano that is common in jazz combos.

Having no piano allows the lead instrument to enjoy more direct interplay between bass and piano. It also places an emphasis on musical lines over harmony. *Compass* borrows this approach from Rollins but ups the ante. Some of its tracks double down on bass and/or drums.

While "Insomnomaniac" swings hard from the very first measure, it is clearly a thoroughly modern piece. There is no melody per se. Instead, the saxophone riffs on a curling, repeating phrase that sounds like a stuck phonograph record. It seems to perfectly reflect the manic mode of a person who cannot fall asleep.

Occasionally, the melody for "Insomnomaniac" loses steam, like a person starting to doze off. This only lasts briefly, though.

Soon, the same manic phrase returns at a higher pitch level, intensifying the mood. The performance follows the outline of a head arrangement, and the band again loses steam at the end of the head.

At this point, the bass introduces a new bluesy riff. Drums soon enter with a shuffling beat. Redman begins his solo by echoing the bass riff but soon veers away from it, blowing jazzy double-time phrases. This does not last for long, though.

As Redman continues to solo, the drums and bass melt out of their bluesy shuffle groove. For a moment even a sense of beat seems to disappear. The three musicians interact with one another freely. When a new groove emerges, it briefly has an Eastern tinge. This, too, soon gives way, with the band breaking into fast straight-ahead playing.

So the solo continues. It does not settle on anything for long. Toward the end, Redman's playing becomes more chaotic. He eventually fades into the background and the drums solo briefly before the piece's manic melody returns.

Vocal Jazz Returns

Improvisation was with me from the beginning. It drove my parents crazy. I would sing all the time. —CASSANDRA WILSON

The jazz revival has brought renewed vitality to vocal jazz. Cassandra Wilson (b. 1955) has been perhaps the most influential artist in this realm. Her early influences included singers Abbey Lincoln and Betty Carter. Concentrating on jazz standards, Wilson developed an ability to scat sing that brings back echoes of Ella Fitzgerald. In 2001, *Time* named her "America's Best

Singer." (By turns, Wilson also draws from outside influences and can be very adventurous.)

Canada's Diana Krall is another important jazz singer to have emerged since the revival. She is also a talented pianist. Krall became one of the most popular jazz artists in the first decade of the

Cassandra Wilson

21st century. She did so by relying heavily on masterful interpretations of jazz standards. After marrying rock star Elvis Costello, Krall also began developing her abilities as a songwriter.

JAZZY STYLISTS

Since the time of Bing Crosby, a string of vocal stylists have brought a jazzy approach to popular music. New Orleans native

Harry Connick, Jr. emerged in the 1980s as the heir to the Las Vegas lounge heritage of Frank Sinatra. He combined a suave air and songwriting skills that have taken him beyond jazz. He has scored a Hollywood movie, *When Harry Met Sally*, and a Broadway musical, *Thou Shalt Not*, and has even developed a career as an actor.

Connick showed that America still had an appetite for jazzy pop singers. Vocalist Jamie Cullum stands as one of the most vocal stylists in the jazz vein today. His recordings sell millions of copies, and he has helped jazz remain popular among young people.

Michael Bublé has enjoyed a career similar to that of Cullum. His crooning sound and rakish demeanor have helped him score hits with a number of jazzy sounding albums. His song "Haven't Met You Yet" even reached #1 on the adult contemporary charts in 2010.

It is just not male artists who have turned to jazz to color their music. American singer-songwriter Norah Jones seemed to come from out of nowhere with her 2002 debut *Come Away With Me*, which sold over 20 million copies for Blue Note—a label historically known for albums by dyed-in-the-wool jazz artists. The crossover appeal of album's relaxed and catchy hit song "Don't Know Why" was remarkable.

The Legacy of the Jazz Revival

In 1980, it was unclear if what we now call straight-ahead jazz would survive. It had lost much of its audience to other popular forms—rock, funk, R&B, and the like. Worse, many jazz musicians seemed to have turned their backs on the legacy of Armstrong, Parker, and Coltrane. In pursuing the fusion music of the

1970s, they appeared to cross over to the popular music camp.

Thanks to the jazz revival, the question of survival for swing-oriented jazz appears to have been answered. Straight-ahead jazz has again flourished since the 1980s. While it is impossible to say for sure that it will never face another moment of threat as it did with fusion, such a thing is hard to imagine.

The revival of jazz has come at somewhat of a cost, though. To a certain extent, it has become a backwards- rather than forward-looking music. They say in Zen Buddhism, "If you meet the Buddha on the road, kill him." It means that we should not hold anything in too much reverence, because it can be stifling. Fortunately, straight-ahead jazz continues to progress in the hands of talented artists like Joshua Redman.

The other legacy of the jazz revival has been the creation of fertile ground for crossover artists like Jamie Cullum and Norah Jones, whose jazz-inflected sounds owe much to the continuing vitality of straight-ahead jazz. They return the favor by introducing jazzy sounds to younger listeners. Some of these fans will certainly begin to explore more authentic forms of jazz, helping keep the tradition alive for another generation.

Trombone Shorty

JAZZ
TODAY

The introduction for this book began at the Chicago Jazz Festival on a balmy, late summer evening. We now jump to a cold January at a small basement club in the Nishiazabu section of Tokyo. The crowd hangs on every cacophonic note pouring from the trio on stage.

This is noise jazz. To many, it does not sound anything like jazz. For some, it does not even sound like music. The guitarist strikes his instrument in jerky movements. There is no melody as such. There is no perceivable form. It is hard to tell if there is a chord progression. Instead, there seems to be a lot of, well, noise.

The sounds of more recognizable forms of jazz fill the air in other Tokyo clubs this evening as well as night spots around the world. In London, Trio Libero is packing them in at Ronnie Scott's. In New Orleans, the Soul Rebels Brass Band is heating things up with a modern take on the traditional brass ensemble. In North Carolina, Bill Hanna is leading a regular jazz jam at Charlotte's Double Door. Jazz seems alive and well.

Soul Rebels Brass Band

In this final chapter, we will consider jazz today. To do so, we'll take a brief look back at the history of the music to understand the present. We'll also ponder where jazz may be headed in the future.

Straight Ahead

In the last chapter, we considered the jazz revival that began in the 1980s. It started as a countermovement to the fusion that prevailed during the previous decade. The revival centered on what has come to be known as straight-ahead jazz. All evidence suggests that the jazz revival has been very successful. The type of jazz it championed is in robust health.

Several traits mark straight-ahead jazz. At its core, we hear the legacy of swing and bebop. A drum typically lays down a swing rhythm while a bass walks underneath and an acoustic piano comps chords. The piano may also serve as the lead instrument. Alternately, we might find a wind instrument like the saxophone or a singer taking the lead.

This type of combo has been the mainstay of jazz since the days of Charlie Parker and Dizzy Gillespie in the 1940s. Today's musicians also continue to favor the sort of head arrangements used by such bebop musicians. They even rely on musical works from earlier generations that now stand as the jazz standards we looked at earlier.

A LIVING TRADITION

A straight-ahead jazz group may also play original works, but they tend to retain some traditional aspects. Jazz is a means for personal expression that respects the past. It is seen as a living tradition, a heritage passed down from Charlie Parker and John Coltrane. Today's musicians embody this tradition while also bringing it into the present. One of the most impressive young players in the straight-ahead vein is John Coltrane's son Ravi.

Programs of study at American high schools and colleges support jazz in several ways, especially straight-ahead varieties. First, they have helped bring legitimacy to the art form. Second, they have served as a refuge for forms of jazz that have lost broad popular appeal. Most important, they have educated a generation of artists. Today, an American jazz musician has more likely learned his art in school then at late-night jam sessions in basement clubs.

Young artists like Troy "Trombone Shorty" Andrews infuse traditional jazz with the energy of rock, bringing showmanship and musicianship together in a way that harkens back to jazz's early days in New Orleans clubs.

Vocalists have been a central part of jazz since the 1920s,

when Louis Armstrong put down his trumpet and started singing. The tradition passed through Billie Holiday and Ella Fitzgerald and has been handed down to modern vocalists like Cassandra Wilson and Diana Krall. A number of other popular singers may not be out-and-out jazz artists, but they do display a jazzy style. Michael Bublé and Norah Jones are two of the most popular.

SUGGESTED LISTENING

DON BYRON
"Tuskegee Strutter's Ball"

RAVI COLTRANE
"Epistrophy"

GURU
"Loungin'"

BONEY JAMES
"The Total Experience"

SONNY SHARROCK
"Many Mansions"
Matthew Shipp
"Nu Bop"

JOHN ZORN/ MASADA
"Jair"

SMOOTH SOUNDS AND FUSION

Looking beyond straight-ahead jazz, we find that smooth sounds continue to be played on radio stations across the country. However, smooth jazz has lately had some problems. A number of the major stations and networks that featured the style have now dropped it. At the same time, the broad appeal of smooth jazz continues. The 2007 album *The Weather Channel Presents: The Best of Smooth Jazz* even reached #1 on Billboard's Contemporary Jazz chart.

Recently, smooth jazz shows signs of merging with the urban contemporary radio format. This features a mix of hip-hop, modern R&B, electronica, and more. Artists who have successfully crossed over from smooth jazz to urban contemporary include Dave Koz and Boney James.

Fusion also lives on. Nowadays, though, it is not so much a movement. It is found more as the concept for a particular album or as a single piece in a largely straight-ahead set played at a jazz club. Fusion compositions like "Chameleon" now even enjoy status as jazz standards.

What was just said about fusion is also largely true for Latin jazz. It is now more one style in an artist's arsenal than music in and of itself. It is something served up to add a little variety to a performance. However, an offshoot of the Cuban jazz movement, salsa, has gone onto to enjoy a life all its own for Latin audiences in American cities like New York and Miami.

Women Step Forward

Women have long been part of jazz. In particular, many jazz singers have been women, including important artists like Ella Fitzgerald and Billie Holiday. For a time, women had fewer opportunities as instrumentalists. Perhaps this had to do with at-

Marian McPartland

titudes that said that instruments like the saxophone and drums were for men rather than women to play.

The piano was an exception. It was considered to be a more acceptable instrument for women, and we can therefore point to a number of early female jazz pianists. They include the legendary Mary Lou Williams and longtime radio host—Marian Mc-Partland. Other instruments had a number of female pioneers as well, like trumpeters Dolly and Valaida Snow. "All girl" big

Esperanza Spalding

bands also enjoyed quite a bit of popularity in the 1940s.

Singing jazz remains a vital form of musical expression for female artists today. Some of today's leading female vocalists include Abbey Lincoln, Cassandra Wilson, Dianne Schurr and Diana Krall. Society now also makes it much more acceptable for anyone to play any instrument. This has led to the recent emergence of women instrumentalists as a force in jazz and has brought new diversity to the form.

Some of the top female instrumentalists leading the way in the 21st century include saxophonists Grace Kelly and Candy Dulfer, drummer Terri Lyne Carrington, flutist Anne Drummond, guitarist Leni Stern, pianist Hiromi, and bassist Esperanza Spalding. In fact, Spalding beat a number of pop stars to win the Best New Artist Grammy in 2011. She is the first jazz artist, male or female, to do so.

That's Jazz?

Jazz has always ignored boundaries in order to move boldly into the future. Often this has taken the form of revolts against established styles. Swing rebelled against traditional jazz. Bebop rose up against swing. Cool jazz took exception to bebop. This pattern has gone on and on throughout the history of jazz, continuing to this day.

Jam bands play with the improvisational openness of jazz but add in grooves and sounds from rock and funk. One of the most popular is the organ, bass/guitar, and drum trio Medeski, Martin, and Wood. They perform and record on their own and have also worked with established jazz artists like guitarist John Scofield.

Nu jazz is one of the latest stylistic trends to challenge more traditional ideas about what jazz is or can be. One sign that the movement is still in a development stage is found in its name.

Medeski, Martin, and Wood

It is also appears as NuJazz and nü-jazz. Some of its alternate names help give us a sense of what it is about—electro-jazz, e-jazz, jazztronica, and even future jazz.

These alternate names for nu jazz reveal it to be plugged-in music. We might then conclude that is a child of 1970s fusion music. There is more to it, though. An international movement, it often combines live performance with the use of looped samples. Nu jazz favors the electronic dance music known as house for its beats.

The French artist St. Germain is one of the leading artists fusing jazz with house beats. Other nu jazz artists show a more obvious connection to modern soul and R&B as well as hip-hop. The music can also be quite experimental, reminding the listener of free jazz.

The Bad Plus

Both the Latin and fusion jazz movements complicated an easy definition of jazz. Before they brought new grooves to the party, one could simply say that jazz was a *style* of music. It combined swinging eighth notes with syncopated rhythms. With the advent of Latin and fusion jazz, that was no longer wholly true.

Even including Latin jazz and fusion, we could still refer to jazz as a musical tradition that emphasizes improvisation. Nu jazz even challenges this bedrock. Critic Tony Brewer has written about nu jazz, "The songs are the focus, not the individual prowess of the musicians." What's left then that makes nu jazz jazz?

Take the trio called the Bad Plus for example: their set list includes songs that were originated by rock artists like Rush, Nirvana, and Black Sabbath. Is their approach all that different from the way the bebop artists reworked songs from musical theater? Today, any song can be turned into a jazz standard by musicians with the right combination of imagination and jazz technique.

MATTHEW SHIPP

Pianist Matthew Shipp has been a leader in the nu jazz world for over a decade. A schooled musician, he studied with the same music teacher, Dennis Sandole, who taught John Coltrane. This musical heritage seems to have inspired his early experiments with free jazz.

From Shipp's 2002 album of the same name, "Nu Bop" is a great example of nu jazz. It starts with a lone soprano saxophone note that morphs into a synthesizer pitch. Acoustic bassist William Parker then enters with a jagged, syncopated riff that is accompanied by a processed drum pattern from Guillermo Barreto Brown. After this musical concoction percolates for a few seconds, the drums drop out only to be replaced by a noisy house beat.

It is more than a minute before a melodic instrument, a saxophone, enters. Even then, there is no melody. The saxophone begins improvising right away in a bebop-like manner. This creates an interesting mix: bebop solo above a house groove. This is definitely nu bop.

After a couple of minutes of soloing, the saxophone and bass drop out, leaving just the drum set. It continues with the house beat, gradually expanding it into a solo. Shipp finally enters four minutes into the performance, playing repetitive, bombastic lines. The saxophone comes back in and solos over Shipp and the house beat for a while longer. Eventually, the band falls away and leaves Shipp pounding away at the piano.

JAZZ RAP

Some recent musical trends involving jazz have come and gone but have left continuing ripples of influence. Jazz rap was a big thing for a while in the 1990s. It was born when rap artists began exploring the grooves on jazz records to use as loops. The marriage of jazz with hip-hop and rap may seem odd. However, some trace the roots of rap all the way back to Louis Armstrong's scat singing on his 1925 recording of "Heebie Jeebies."

LIVES AND TIMES

Yuppies By the 1980s, most baby boomers had abandoned counterculture ideas. They reengaged with mainstream values in the 1980s and many emerged as "young urban professionals," yuppies for short. As they did, they rediscovered more traditional aspects of American life, including jazz.

The Internet In the 1990s, America and the rest of the world started to go online. For jazz artists, it meant a way for them to connect with audiences more directly. For jazz fans, it meant almost instant access to the entire history of jazz as a recorded art form.

Jazz rap as a genre pretty much began with the 1985 single "Jazz Rap" by British jazz musician Mike Carr. In 1988, Carr followed up with "Words I Manifest," a release that sampled Dizzy Gillespie's recording of "A Night in Tunisia."

The 1991 album *The Low End Theory* by A Tribe Called Quest helped put jazz rap on the map. Critic Oliver Wang noted that the album showed that jazz and hip-hop "originated from the same black center." *Rolling Stone* magazine added, "Hip-hop and jazz—both were revolutionary forms of black music based in improvisation and flow—but A Tribe Called Quest's second album drew the entire picture."

Jazz rap hit a high point in 1993 with Digable Planets' 1993 album *Reachin'* (*A New Refutation of Time and Space*). It sampled such jazz masters as Sonny Rollins, Art Blakey, and Herbie Hancock. The album's single "Rebirth of Slick (Cool Like Dat)" placed high on the charts and received extensive airplay.

A HIP-HOP INFLUENCE

Such music clearly shows the influence of jazz on hip-hop artists. The inspiration went both ways, though. Jazz stalwarts like Herbie Hancock and Branford Marsalis released albums laced with rap and hip-hop. Even the legendary Miles Davis turned to hip-hop for his final album.

The rapper Guru helped jazz rap remain vibrant into the 21stcentury. His series of *Jazzmatazz* recordings brought a who's who of jazz artists to record in the studio with him, including trumpeters Freddie Hubbard and Donald Byrd, as well as Herbie Hancock.

Jazz rap has largely faded as a movement. It can still be heard now and then in the music of certain artists. The Roots is one of the main groups continuing to explore jazz rap. The rapper Kayne West also sampled saxophonist Joe Farrell's "Upon This Rock" in his 2008 "Gone."

FUTURISM

We sometimes find jazz today blended with other forms of music beyond rap. This is a clear legacy of the 1970s fusion movement. While fusion mixed jazz with rock and funk, today we also find concoctions with more unusual elements. Noise jazz is one of the most exotic of these.

Futurism was an artistic movement that developed in Italy in the early part of the 20th century. It found much inspiration in modern technology. Composer Luigi Russolo extended futurist ideas to music with his 1913 manifesto, *The Art of Noise.* He claimed that industrialization had given people an appreciation for more complex sounds.

Noise artists have been putting Russolo's claim to the test for the better part of a century. A noise work typically consists of sounds produced by an object or objects not usually considered to be musical. The sounds may be altered electronically. If traditional musical instruments are used, they are played in non-traditional ways. For example, a performer might stomp on an electric guitar or bang on the soundboard of a piano, even reach in and strum its strings.

NOISE ROCK

In the late 1960s, rock artists like John Lennon of the Beatles and John Cale of the Velvet Underground were inspired by avant-garde music, in particular, noise. Then, in 1975, rocker Lou Reed, who had also been in the Velvet Underground, released his album *Metal Machine Music.* Considered by some to be a joke, its mixture of rock and noise was also hailed by some critics.

Noise rock started taking on more and more of a punk flavor in the 1980s with groups like Sonic Youth and Mission of Burma. From the 1970s on, a number of musicians also explored the possibilities of combining noise with jazz. In particular, they built on the musical foundation laid by free jazz in the 1960s. Guitarist Sonny Sharrock was an early pioneer of noise jazz; for decades guitarist and composer Elliott Sharp has also explored its possibilities.

According to guitarist Michael Simon, today's "noise jazz musicians play together with few or no rules, and thus are free to follow their feelings." Where is the jazz in noise jazz then? As with fusion and free jazz, it is found in the basic orientation of the musicians. Despite all the noise, the listener can still sense that artistically the artists are coming from a jazz "place."

A number of today's artists display a jazz heritage but seem to defy further categorization. One example is saxophonist and clarinetist Don Byron. His musical exploits have ranged from

Don Byron

the Jewish dance music known as klezmer and the compositions of cartoon soundtrack composer Raymond Scott to hip-hop and even a bold reconceptualization of the music of classical composer Gustav Mahler.

The music of saxophonist John Zorn and trumpeter Dave Douglas, both composers, also confounds categorization. Beginning the 1990s, they fronted the band Masada. According to Zorn, "The idea with Masada is to produce a sort of radical Jewish music." The works for the group were also obviously inspired by free jazz. Again, to quote Zorn, "The idea is to put Ornette Coleman and the Jewish scales together."

Zorn and Douglas have each also pursued a range of musically diverse projects before and since the group's founding. In terms of improvisation, Zorn has continued a longstanding interest in drawing from many different sources ranging from cartoon music to birdcalls, both in improvisation and composition.

With his Keystone sextet — which includes electric bass and turntables in addition to more standard jazz instruments, Douglas plays music inspired by new and old films; he also leads a number of other groups that are more traditional, at least in terms of instrumentation, including a classic quintet, a big band, and even a brass ensemble, Brass Ecstasy.

The Future of Jazz

Jazz has been around for almost a hundred years now. It is remarkable that the musical sounds first heard in the Storyville section of New Orleans became *the* music of America. It is all the more remarkable that the echoes of those strains still resound so loudly in many different forms, and they do so around the world.

There were a few times in the history of jazz that it might have disappeared. The onslaught of rock 'n' roll in the 1950s changed American tastes in music. Jazz suffered as a result. The fusion movement of the 1970s presented its own threat by replacing swing as the rhythmic style of jazz with rock and funk.

The jazz revival that started in the 1980s has helped assure that jazz will continue long into the future. In fact, it is hard to imagine it ever being severely threatened again. In part, this is because jazz is now bolstered by an educational system to train new generations of musicians.

Recognition of jazz as an important art form also helps ensure its continued existence. A number of important documentaries on its history have been produced, most notably Ken Burns' series for public television. The United States government has proclaimed the music's value in American life. Many jazz artists now also find support from grant-awarding organizations, ranging from local arts councils to the National Endowment for the Arts.

An increase in the venues and media that support jazz is helping the music prosper into the 21st century as well. Established jazz festivals are found in many cities, and the Internet allows jazz artists to reach fans directly whether they live in Kansas or Katmandu. Online sales of jazz recordings as MP3 files through such sites as iTunes and Amazon.com have also helped make the music more widely available.

One other thing helps ensure that jazz will remain an important music well into the future. As proclaimed in this book's introduction, jazz is what America aspires to be. It emphasizes individualism and spontaneous creation in a way that clearly embodies the American motto *e pluribus unum*. As long as it does so, Americans will continue to embrace it and jazz will inspire musicians and fans around the world.

APPENDIX

WEB SITES AND MAGAZINES

Downbeat Magazine: downbeat.com

Jazz.com: jazz.com

The Red Hot Jazz Archive: redhotjazz.com

Jazz Online: jazzonline.com

JAZZIZ Magazine: jazziz.com

JazzTimes Magazine: jazztimes.com

FESTIVALS

Chicago Jazz Festival (Chicago, IL)

Essentially Ellington High School Jazz Band Competition and Festival (New York, NY)

JVC Jazz Festival (New York, NY)

Monterey Jazz Festival (Monterey, CA)

New Orleans Jazz & Heritage Festival (New Orleans, LA)

Newport Jazz Festival (Newport, RI)

Notre Dame Collegiate Jazz Festival (Notre Dame, IN)

Playboy Jazz Festival (Los Angeles, CA)

MUSEUMS, ARCHIVES AND ORGANIZATIONS

American Jazz Museum (Kansas City, MO)

Chicago Jazz Archive at University of Chicago (Chicago, IL)

Hogan Jazz Archive at Tulane University (New Orleans, LA)

Jazz Archive at Duke University (Duke, NC)

National Jazz Museum in Harlem (New York, NY)

Smithsonian Jazz at National Museum of American History (Washington, DC)

Jazz at Lincoln Center (www.jazzatlincolncenter.org

REFERENCES

The Rough Guide to Jazz 3 (Rough Guide Reference) by Ian Carr, Digby Fairweather and Brian Priestley. Rough Guides, 2004.

The Penguin Jazz Guide: The History of the Music in the 1001 Best Albums by Brian Morton and Richard Cook. Penguin, 2010.

All Music Guide to Jazz : The Definitive Guide to Jazz Music by Vladimir Bogdanov, Chris Woodstra and Stephen Thomas Erlewine. Backbeat Books, 2002.

DOCUMENTARIES

Jazz: A Film By Ken Burns. PBS, 2001.

Jazz on a Summer's Day. New Yorker, 2000.

Lady Day - The Many Faces of Billie Holiday. White Star, 2000.

Masters of American Music: The Story of Jazz. Euroarts, 2009.

COLLEGE JAZZ PROGRAMS

Berklee College of Music

Eastman School of Music

University of North Texas

University of Miami

University of Southern California

Western Michigan University

WORKSHOPS AND CAMPS

Berklee College of Music Summer Programs (Boston, MA)

Eastman Summer Jazz Studies (Rochester, NY)

Interlochen High School Jazz Summer Program (Interlochen, MI)

Jamey Aebersold's Summer Jazz Workshops (Louisville, KY)

JazzCamp WEST (La Honda, CA)

useum

PHOTO CREDITS

Courtesy of the Hogan Jazz Archive, Tulane University: Jelly Roll Morton, pg.14

William P. Gottlieb Collection/Library of Congress: Louis Armstrong, pg. 30; Benny Goodman, pg. 44; Lionel Hampton, pg. 52; Gene Krupa, pg. 54; Tommy Dorsey and Beryl Davis, pg. 56; Ellington and Basie, pg. 60; Duke Ellington, pg. 66; Basie, pg. 73; Charlie Parker, pg.76 ; Milt Jackson, pg. 89; Ella Fitzgerald, pg. 92; Billie Holiday, pg. 103 ; Frank Sinatra, pg. 107; Jose Mangual, Machito, and Carlos Vidal, pg. 108; Xavier Cugat, pg. 111; Dizzy Gillespie, pg. 114

Don Hunstein © Sony Music Entertainment: Charkie Rouse and Thelonius Monk, pg. 87; Stan Getz, pg. 122; Dave Brubeck, pg. 124; Gerry Mulligan pg. 132; Charles Mingus, pg. 138; John Coltrane and Miles Davis, pg. 144; Miles Davis, pg. 148; John Coltrane, pg. 158; Jaco Pastorius, pg. 160; Weather Report, pg. 165; Return To Forever, pg. 169

Urve Kuusik © Sony Music Entertainment: John McLaughlin, pg. 172

Sony Music Archives: Herbie Hancock, pg. 171

ICONS: PhotoObjects.net/thinkstock, pg. xv, pg. 109; **comstock/thinkstock,** pg. 2, pg. 15, pg. 45; **istockphoto/thinkstock,** pg. 31, pg. 93, pg. 161, pg. 179; **stockbyte/thinkstock,** pg. 61, pg. 77; **Hemera/thinkstock,** pg. 125, pg. 195; **AbleStock.com/thinkstock,** p. 145

Infrogmation: Preservation Hall Jazz Band, pg. 26; **Chuck Stewart:** John and Alice Coltrane, pg. 155; **Jimmy Katz:** Pat Metheny, pg. 174; **Clay Patrick McBride at Anderson Hopkins:** Wynton Marsalis, cover, pg. 178; **Frank Stewart:** Cassandra Wilson, pg. 191; **Jenny Bagert:** Terrence Blanchard, pg. 185; **Jane Richey:** Trombone Shorty, pg. 194; **Johann Sauty:** Esparanza Spalding, pg. 200; **Cameron Wittig:** The Bad Plus, pg. 202

PRESS: Big Bad Voodoo Daddy, pg. xiv; Ornette Coleman, pg. 140; Mindi Abair, pg. 177; Dirty Dozen Brass Band, pg. 181; Joshua Redman, pg. 188; Soul Rebels Brass Band, pg. 196; Marian McPartland, pg. 199; Medeski, Martin and Wood, pg. 201; Don Byron, pg. 207

James E. Taylor, Frank Leslie's Illustrated Newspaper, vol. 24, no. 601 (6 April, 1867), pg.17

INDEX